She w... Boat
Please e...
or keep
Liz or Betty

Potpourri
KATHRYN SOJKA-FAIRCHILD

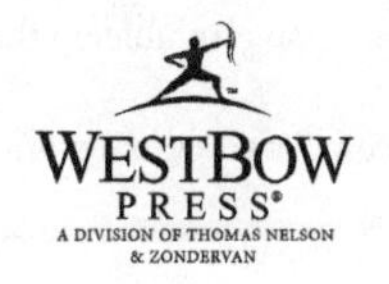
WESTBOW
PRESS®
A DIVISION OF THOMAS NELSON
& ZONDERVAN

WestBow Press books may be ordered through booksellers or by contacting:

WestBow Press
A Division of Thomas Nelson & Zondervan
1663 Liberty Drive
Bloomington, IN 47403
www.westbowpress.com
1 (866) 928-1240

ISBN: 978-1-9736-4039-4 (sc)
ISBN: 978-1-9736-4037-0 (hc)
ISBN: 978-1-9736-4038-7 (e)

Library of Congress Control Number: 2018911248

Print information available on the last page.

WestBow Press rev. date: 5/31/2019

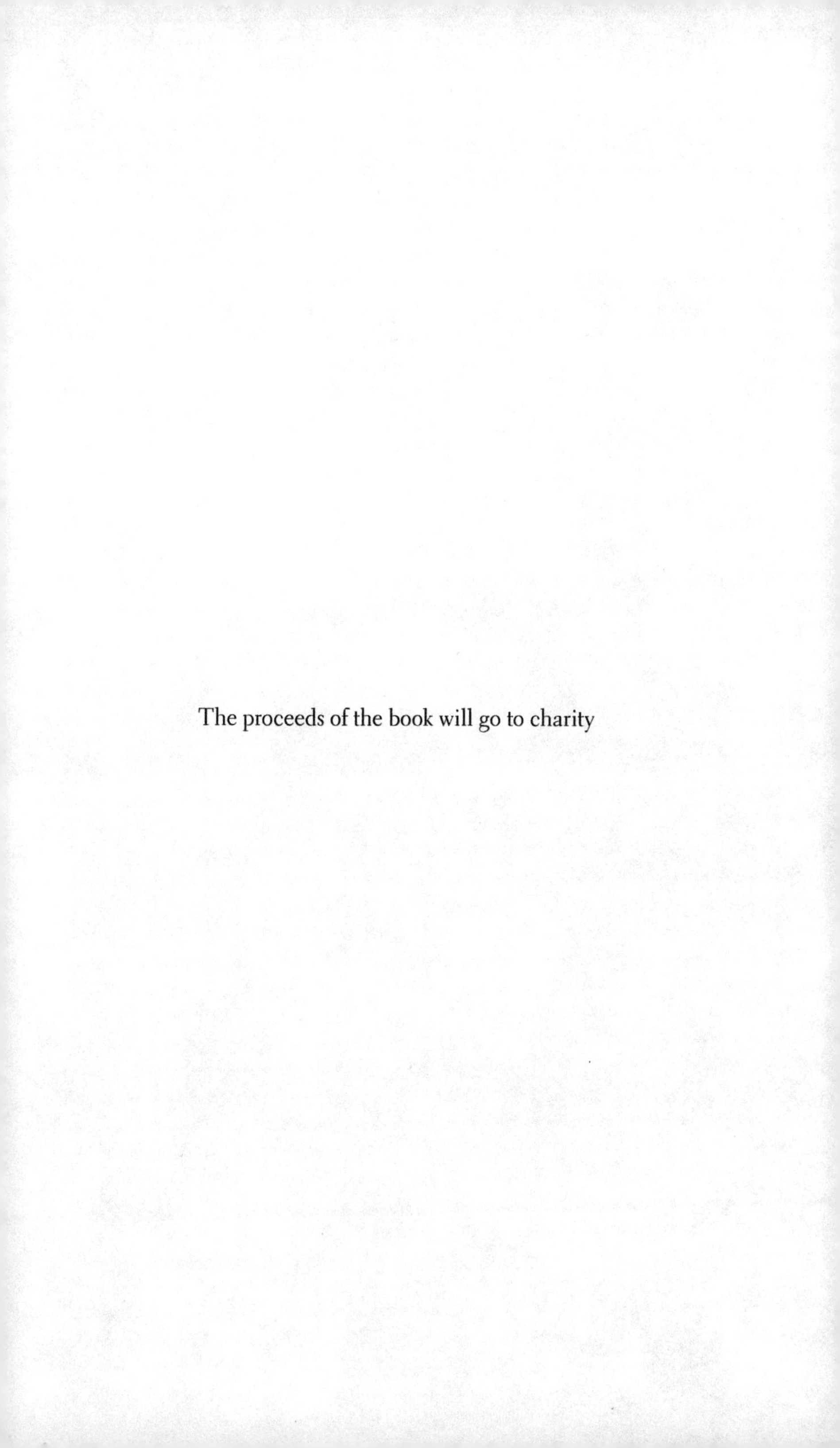

The proceeds of the book will go to charity

This book is dedicated with great joy to
Lisa, Laura and Daniela Sojka,
my daughters-in-law.

I feel that my sons
by their marriages
chose my daughters for me.

Good Job Guys!
I admire and love them so much.
Your taste in women is unsurpassed.*

*(You inherited your amazing taste in women from your Dad!)

Until you can put your feelings
into words, give them form,
they're like smoke, swirling all around.
You can't grab them, hold onto them
and make them something of substance.
It's also a way to reach inside
and find out what's in there.

And, so I write and write and write.

Now, about my poetry,
English teachers and others,
both literate and literary
will, no doubt,
kneel before the gods of iambic pentameter
.... sobbing! ....

The words come just the way
They are inside me,
without refinement or proper form.
So,yes I understand
That it's not perfected ...
it just IS.

Sometimes a working out of something.
Sometimes taking a surprising twist or turn
even to me.
I'm compelled to write, so I'm glad I enjoy it.
The gratifying surprise
was that others enjoyed what I wrote.

.... I had many kinds
of sounds ringing in my ears and
they sometimes asked to get on paper.

THOMAS MERTON
(The Seven Story Mountain)

THIS 'N THAT

BY- KATHRYN SOJKA-FAIRCHILD

It's My Life; So What?

Power was
in his hands, you see.
He thought he was the
pinnacle of what to be.

Arrogance crept in
as a daily thought.
And if he should sin—
so what? So what?

Time from his family
he did cut:
ignored his children.
So what? So what?

Cheated on his taxes.
(He thinks everybody does!)
His way was the only way—
a brain filled with fuzz.

Alas, alack,
he got old.
His only comfort
was his gold.

Life was over,
and he went to hell.
So what? So what?
There's no more to tell.

As I was going through some things, I found the words to a song I wrote after a girlfriend dared me. She said that I could not write about being addicted to alcohol since I don't drink. Here it is:

The Old-Time Alcohol Blues

My hands are a-shakin';
My nerves are a mess.
My kids hate me,
And I couldn't care less.
Help me, O Lord.
I can't afford Betty Ford.

My wife's leavin',
And she's takin' the dawg.
The cat bit me;
My brain's in a fog.
Help me, O Lord.
I can't afford Betty Ford.

I got a beer belly.
It's an awful sight.
Days are a blur;
It's worse at night.
Help me, O Lord.
I can't afford Betty Ford.

I drove on the sidewalk yesterday.
They're going to take my license away.
My life's getting worse and worse.
Almost as bad as all this verse!
Help me, O Lord.
I can't afford Betty Ford.

My girlfriend laughed and conceded.

A Young Woman

Woman-child
walks in wonder
of herself,
changes, and of life.
Trying on ideas
like a dress,
examining front and back.
Clutching a few, discarding others.
Looking with critical eye at some,
embracing others with little thought.
Walking a line between
little girl and woman,
she dashes back and forth
with joyous abandon,
with trepidation,
and sometimes with fear.

Dichotomy

What frightening forces men control.
The atom they can split.
(How very few know how to create
a family that's close-knit.)

The sound barrier they do break;
weighty minds do play a part.
(No formula's ever been devised
to unbreak the human heart.)

They can fly and walk upon
the silvery, far distant moon.
(Will ever man devise a plan
to make a boy clean his room?)

They've solved the puzzle of the age.
DNA they took apart.
(No one's ever understood
the depths of a mother's heart.)

Nature Noir

Sin is a spider web,
and
we are the fly,
imprisoned in the web's deceiving beauty.
Its intricacy, its form draws us near.
Our eyes, our minds seem drawn to it
in exciting increments.
This pseudo-beauty, this subtleness draws us near.
Its beauty hides the delusion, the illusion
that this is something
we must have, have to have,
and we have bought the lie.
The beauty cloaks the real intent,
which is drawing us toward
judgment and death.

August

I went into a store today.
They had Christmas on display!
Rushing, rushing, rushing time.
Do they need another dime?
Taking the sacred, the divine.
Rushing, rushing, rushing time.
September, October, November, December.
Excitement depleted when comes the day.
Sacred gone (to my dismay).
Can't Christmas have its special time?
Rushing, rushing, rushing time.

Courtesy Is Just a Nice Way to Get Along

What has happened
to kindness and grace?
Where is the smile
that belongs on your face?

Where is "thank you"?
Where is "please"?
Oh! Please cover your mouth
when you sneeze!

Thank you notes
and RSVPs
have gone by the wayside
as far as I can see.

A man opened a door for me and said,
"Here you go, miss."
I wanted to grab him
and give him a kiss!

(Instead, I just said, "Thank you!")

The Owl

Eyes piercing the dark,
scanning the earth as it soars.
Wings silently gliding
o'er the dusk and dark trees.
Signaling the night of its presence
by its haunting refrain of *hoo-ooot.*
Such beauty hidden by the blackness,
seen in shadow and outline.
Does it hide its majesty from us
or deem us unworthy
its splendor to behold?

A Different Dimension

Is that a breeze?
Or is God passing by?
For the flowers are gently
bowing as if in worship.

Is that a bird song I hear?
Or is it a fragment of an angel's voice
as he sings in praise
of our God?

Is that the sun's warmth I feel?
Or is that warmth within me
the essence of love
as the Holy Spirit makes Himself known?

Are those clouds I see?
Or is their billowing whiteness
reflecting off the wings
of angels?

Is that rain I see?
Or is it the combined tears of all the angels
as they see many souls
unknowing of God?

The Media Has the Megaphone

What we think.
What we do.
What to wear.
To buy that shoe.

How to reason.
How to think.
What to eat.
What to drink.

You can't believe that!
We'll stop you!
We'll give you a label:
at least one or two.

Think what we think.
Do what we do.
Stand for morality?
How could you?

We'll laugh at you,
make you a freak
at six o'clock,
week after week.

Tradition

A pickle or a pear.
A pear or a pickle.
Who would make a fuss
and be so fickle
as to care if he got
a pickle or a pear,
a pear or a pickle
on a Christmas tree
to hide and giggle
with a reach and wink,
a toss and a wiggle.
If you find this fruit,
then you get the loot
of an extra gift
on Christmas day.

I have no idea where or how this Christmas tradition started or how it relates to the meaning of the holiday. This was in my 2004 Christmas card for Lindsay and Kelly Fairchild, who first told me about this tradition.

Newspapers

Page after page,
it screams,
"Death!
Fear!
Violence!
Rage and grief!"
Becoming an effort
to turn each page
as you read on
from story to story,
slogging through
statistics, body counts.
Acts of violence,
chaos,
blinding grief
jump from the pages
as survivors mourn.

GOD

You are the only thing that makes sense.
My path is set before me.
I must learn, grow, pray, love
to ensure my escape
from the
madness!

My peace lies in You.

Me, Important?

Most of our lives
resemble a sigh.
We stir the air,
and we pass on,
leaving history undisturbed.
A birth, a generation, death,
and most of us
never even ruffle
the pages of life.
An instant—gone,
from birth to death
held up against eternity.
Our time here
is barely a blink of any eye.
So why do we think
we are so important,
that what we want
is so important?

THIRTY-
THREE
YEARS

Always a King

The first to be drawn to Him were shepherds
drawn by the light of a star,
though the rest of the world was in spiritual darkness.
He was not a prince in this world
(even though He was the Prince of peace),
but He was always a King.
Shepherds may have been called to be witnesses
because they were humble and poor.
They had no worldly attitude—
maybe a litmus test for us as to what our attitudes
toward life and our fellow human are to be.
Wise men were also called,
perhaps to show that wisdom is always in the presence
of this King of kings and Lord of lords.
A single star hovered over the birth,
announcing that this King is the light of the world.
The riches of earthly kings are as dust
compared to the riches of our Creator.
The richness of our lives in and with Him
surpasses all the world can offer.
He calls us His children!
He tells us He is our Father!
"Surely Goodness and Mercy will follow us
all the days of our lives and
we will dwell in the house of the Lord forever."

Scripture speaks: "Surely goodness and mercy will follow us all the days of our lives and we will dwell in the house of the Lord forever" (Psalm 23:6).

Righteous Anger

Did He storm into the temple,
or did He
quietly and with determination
firmly tread?

Is this something He looked down upon from heaven.
Or was it what He happened upon
when He was twelve and teaching
in His Father's holy place?

Seeing a house of prayer made into a den of thieves—
God's house, where His children gathered to worship Him.

Did He look upon deception
and sin
in people's lives
with horror or compassion?

A warning to future generations
that yes, God is love,
but He is holy
and commands respect.

God is present.
He is God.
He is holy.
He is all.

He gave us life and beauty
to surround us in our daily lives.
He is all.
He is the source of all things.

Be humble, for He works through the foolish
to confound the wise.

"Has not God made foolish the wisdom of the world?" (1 Corinthians 1:20)
"For the wisdom of the world is foolish in God" (1 Corinthians 3:19).

He Was; He Did

He went among the people,
The great unwashed.
He initially gathered humble, uneducated,
Simple men around Him.
Those with open hearts, open minds.
Men used to earning their keep
By the sweat of their brows.
He walked among the blind, deaf, the lame,
The crippled, the young, the old.
Saints, sinners, thieves, but not among men of influence—yet.
The great outdoors were His lecture hall.
Drawing His followers by love, truth, gentleness,
His love for the Father.
His presence was little noted by those in charge—yet.
There was teaching. Then the preaching.
The teaching and preaching became one and the same.
Murmuring started.
Whispering to and among the religious leaders of the day.
They began to see His influence, His charisma.
They began to fear loss of their power, their influence.
They were made uneasy
As He gently taught that the spirit of the law
Was more important than the letter of the law.
His calmness in the face of their spitefulness threatened them.
Troubling were the miracles, healings, the gift of hope.
He taught us to love one another and to love God.
He opened the eyes of the heart, the mind, and
Taught that love was supreme yet the handmaiden of obedience.
With dignity, He fulfilled His purpose.
He was aware of the maneuvering, the growing anxiety
And hatred gathering in those in authority.
He calmly challenged their intentions.
They feared His gentleness, His unfailing integrity, His concern for the people,
His total love for the Father, His truth.
As always, the murmuring, the plotting swirled around Him,
Growing more hateful and bold as plans were surreptitiously made,
Growing more hateful and bold as their fear of Him increased.

Aware of this opposition, He continued gently and faithfully
the work of His Father.
Jesus knew what His fate was to be,
and wanting every moment, every word, every action
to be faithful to the Will of the Father,
He took time apart and fell to His knees before the Father
to affirm His faithfulness, His love, His obedience.
Hate, fed by jealousy and fear, grew and sinister plans
escaped back rooms and secret meetings and were now out in the open.
Betrayed by one of His own, who brought the soldiers
with a crowd following, seeking to be a part of the spectacle.
At the moment of betrayal, the humiliation, imagine the fear
of His disciples being in the eye of the tornado of confusion and panic.
What was to become of them?
Feel their terror and confusion seeing their Beloved
at the mercy of mere men? How could this be?
He, who was without Sin, took all of mankind's Sin upon Himself!
Can you imagine the horror of taking upon Himself, the filth of our Sin?
He, who was righteousness itself.
He, who was clothed in the white garments of Purity.
He, who is Divine, always at the right hand of the Father.
He experienced holy Goodness and Love from the Father.
and was Goodness and Love.
He poured out Himself for us.
By His obedience and love, He endured and
by His Body and Blood He bought Eternal Life for us.

And some still know Him not or even acknowledge His existence.

JOHN 15:13 ... Greater love has no one than this, that one lay down his life for his friends.

Matthew 20:28 ... The Son of Man did not come to be served, but to serve and give His life as a ransom for many.

MARK 10:45 ... For even the Son of Man did not come to be served, but to serve and to give His life as a ransom for many.

JOHN 10:28 ... I give them eternal life and they shall never perish and no one can snatch them out of My hand.

1 JOHN 3:16 ... This is how we know what love is: Jesus Christ laid down His life for us.

BLOOD ON THE STONES

His blood is on the stones.
Blood of the Lamb of God.
Falling drop by agonizing drop
As the thorns are pushed into His head.
And the flogging;
Blood splatter flies as if bowlfuls are flung.
Yes, the flogging:-
Flesh rips and hangs and falls exposing bone.
The crowd is transfixed at the horror. Yet they stay.
Some look away.
Can anything be sadder than innocent blood shed?
Can anything be more horrendous than the fact
That mankind dared even touch their Creator?
Dared to mock Him, spit on Him, hit Him,
Pull out His beard!
Wind, rain and foot traffic over the blood
Seem to wear it away, grind it away as time goes by.
Though unseen, it will forever remain.
For this is holy ground.

And we must never forget.

LIGHT

Jesus is the "Light of the World"
It's a Light we don't always see.
We block this Light and stumble through Darkness.
(How stupid, how pitiful are we?)

A blessing of riches we pass right by.
Looking away from the Light.
We peer into Darkness and cling to the belief,
What's wrong can't be made right.

Each of us can make a difference.
Raise your voice, uplift your thoughts.
We can be Light*, we can be Salt.*
In the morass of sin we need not be caught.

We're not helpless and we matter.
We can and should stand tall.
Do unto others *not* as they do.
Love is important, Love is all.

Scripture speaks:
Mt: 5:13 You are the salt of the earth
Mt: 5:14 You are the light of the world.

THE
WAY I
SEE IT

NINE ELEVEN

Gone is innocence.
It's been taken from you.
When those planes crashed into buildings,
it was torn from Red, White and Blue.

Fellow citizens falling from buildings.
They jumped rather than faced the fire.
Our hearts were well and fully broken.
We were wrenched into sorrow, anger and ire.

Fellow humans across the world
live under clouds of blood.
Hearts and minds twisted.
Hate bursts into flames, insanity floods.

We always knew there were bad people.
But it took 9-11 to teach
that Evil lives among us.
No one's beyond its' reach.

Our call number for help is Nine-one-one.
Who knew in our history it would proclaim
unreasonable, unimagined violence.
Hate and destruction was the aim.

We can never reclaim those pieces
Never reclaim those lives.
Our hearts have a piece missing.
Part of our soul still cries.

Across the world an inferno
Where old men tend the flame.
Young men on their limited piece of sand
Claim martyrdom attached to their name.

We know light overcomes darkness.
When and where we all want to know.
Will the twisted hate in their hearts find completion
Will they be willing to let it go?

Hate burns so fiercely.
Will it someday consume all?
Can we all return to civilized lives?
Or will we descend collectively into the final fall?

Let us face the future with courage.
We're the land of the free and the brave.
We've turned from God and our values.
His Commandments only will save.

We must turn back to our Founders' viewpoints.
Our God-given inalienable rights.
With rights come responsibilities.
Our nation's foundation seems to crumble overnight.

Arrogance and immorality become de riguer.
It seems nothing is wrong anymore, so sad, so true.
We no longer stand as the good, the right,
Here in the Red, White and Blue.

TRED LIGHTLY

Upon our bodies there are signs;
wrinkles, lines and scars that tell a story.
Proceed with caution as you interact with others,
for many carry wounds and scars unseen
upon their hearts, minds and emotions.
You never know what bruises or scars are still new, still healing.
You are not the only one who walks with unseen pain.
Walk with care.
Life has many ways to inflict pain
And you don't want to add
to the pain that accompanies others.
Take care.
There are millions who go through their day as the
"walking wounded"
You may not see or hear or notice their pain.
So ....
Tred lightly as you go through your day.
You don't want to add your footprints on their hearts.

IF

If wishes could be dishes
We could put on a shelf,
to be ignored until it was time
for them to come into use.

If love was tangible,
Struggled to see truth
And brought us insights,
We would have wisdom.

If wants would be only for needs,
wouldn't it be a world less greedy,
less envious, more satisfied?

Meditate on this
And comprehend that:
Less leads to More.

GOSSIP

Wagging tongues in nodding heads
as if they're in "the know."
Tongues as swords
slashing reputations.
Seeing others' faults,
but are they perfection?
With not enough to do
they mind their neighbors' business.
A nasty habit puts them in danger
of becoming nasty people.

If you do things differently than me,
do I become the enemy?

MYTHICAL MUSINGS

The Unicorn is a symbol
of innocence and purity.
I'm convinced that's why
the Unicorn is now extinct.

I'm convinced that last one died
at a junior high school
somewhere in California.

(think about it)

(OR ...... on reality t.v.)

IN MARRIAGE...............

Remember that kindness is more powerful than criticism.

That gentleness has greater power than a fist.

A smile, a touch, a moment of kindness and encouragement are the greatest investment you can make in your marriage and your personal happiness.

If you stop nurturing, you stop loving.

A whisper often can be heard better than a shout.

If someone is not listened to, not heard, the pain it causes makes them feel as if they are dying because it seems they no longer exist.

When you don't stand up for your partner, it's a betrayal and a knife in your partner's heart.

Some people stand silently by and watch the life drain out of the most important relationship of their life and then wonder, "What happened"?

People understand that plants must be fed and watered or they will die, but often fail to understand that a marriage must also be fed and nurtured or it, too, will die.

Without romance, wiping toothpaste off the mirror and picking up dirty socks becomes resentment. It's no longer something you do out of love, it just becomes another chore to get done.

AWAY FROM YOU

There's a whirlwind in the world
and it's faster and faster.
Caught in its' spiral, mankind is being
pulled away from You, our Center.

The hate, fear and violence
on Earth
seems to hurry us towards madness.
We are caught in the vortex.

Insanity, violence, lust for power
fills the air and heats the blood
of those who would kill.
Not knowing their own soul is dying.

No honor, only brutality
and rabid opinions fiercely held.
Vituperation is their song.
They feel powerful, not knowing they're insane.

The color is red:
all the blood shed
by the
Innocent.

God's hands hover around
and cup the Earth
and the Universe hears
a whispered "WOE".

HUMAN RACE

Racing here,
racing there
Racing nearly
everywhere.

So much to do,
So much to see,
Stop and smell roses?
How can that be?

Can't enjoy the moment.
Can't stop this pace.
I'm being sucked into
the human race.

Enjoy tomorrow?
Enjoy today?
Don't have the time!
Get outta' my way!

Got to achieve.
Got to do.
The world can't move
without me! It's true!

I'm important.
Got to keep the pace..
Can't let down
The human race.

THE TIMES THEY ARE A'CHANGING

Entitled mentality,
changing life for all.
No kindness, no courtesy.
Hearts and minds of all.
Loving neighbors as yourself,
seems no longer true.
Making life less pleasant
in the red, white and blue.
Do our hearts swell when we see the flag?
Standing with hands over heart?
No, we sit, we ignore, we chatter.
Patriotism, plays no part.
Violence programmed in computer games.
A tutorial for our kids.
Madness and mayhem entertaining now.
We teach when we buy such "vids".
If you have values, morals.
If you believe in God.
You are now fair game
for taunts and insults from the mob.
We now are not to comment on color.
We're moving towards ignoring race.
But if you are religious.
Crude comments, insults are okay, are in place.
Respect? Courtesy?
Are extinct (or fading) it seems.
Kindness and Graciousness?
We've changed our nation's themes.
No streets of Gold, No Freedom
are in our immigrants dreams.
Insults and name calling
are emerging now it seems.
Respect, Courtesy, Integrity
must come forward and make a stand.
Across Mountain, Prairie, Sea and Shore
of this greatest land.

THE MANY WAYS OF LOVE

Love comes softly,
and draws you close.
It surrounds and
becomes part of you.
It sings in your heart,
yet is the most gentle silence.
Love knows.
Love fulfills.
Love is closest
to Heaven you can be.
Love your Family..
Love your Neighbors.
Love Yourself.
Most of all,
LOVE GOD
as this will expand to
love for all
who come into your Life.

ETERNAL

We wonder …

What can last forever?

The Trinity: Father, Son & Holy Spirit.
The Word of God.
The Souls of people.

As we look at these words, we wonder.
If these things are eternal,
how much attention do we pay them
in our day to day lives?

We are on a journey,
but are we on the right path?

MURDER IS AGAINST STATE AND FEDERAL LAW SO WHAT'S THE PROBLEM?

A friend and I have been having an interesting and meaningful on-going discussion recently about abortion. I describe the dialogue this way because it is just that-a discussion, not an argument.

His view is that we have no right to tell someone that they are required to carry a baby to full term.

My view is that now scientists all agree: that life begins at conception. If abortion stops a beating heart, then how is this not killing? And if I stand up and say that killing is wrong, that murder is wrong, how can I be faulted for standing up for what I believe in?

When did we stop having to be responsible for our actions? You might say that I am Pro-Choice, but for me that choice is 9 months before a birth when you choose to engage in behavior that results in the consequences of your actions.

I had a neighbor who worked in an abortion clinic. She said when saline solution was used to terminate pregnancy that the babies come out looking as if they were screaming. I understand that some babies are vacuumed out piece by piece.

If, in this free country, I am not allowed to voice my beliefs then be afraid, for you will be next. You will find that you have no right to voice your opinions either.

The Ten Commandments are not "ten suggestions." Looking pragmatically at them it seems as if you follow their teaching you will keep many problems out of your life. If, that is, you are allowed to have a life.

ME,
MYSELF
AND I

AUTOBIOGRAPHY

Ponder, ponder as I wonder
what is the meaning of life?
I've been a daughter, sister, mother
and twice I've been a wife!

I've never sailed the Seven Seas,
nor given mother-daughter teas.
Nor para-sail, delivered the mail,
blazed a trail or eaten a snail.

In a helicopter over a beach
dancing waves out of my reach.
A 30 knot wind shook me a bunch
and when I landed, I lost my lunch.

In a basket
under a balloon,
my son and I
flew close to the moon.

The Arctic Circle
I have crossed.
In the West Indies ocean,
I've been tossed.

A personal plane I've been in.
Committed more than my share of sin.
Now I find that I'm growing old
and being a Grandma is pure gold!

(Welcome, Sofia Marie!)

THERE WAS A TIME WHEN I WAS THE MOTHER OF THREE TEENAGERS!

Listen to Life's whispers.
Tiptoe through a day.
Spend time in your "quiet."
These moments mustn't get away.
Noise makes us feel too busy
to reflect and think, to cease.
Make space in the whirlwind
for quiet and rest and peace.

REALIZATION

I suffer when I think
of the Wounds
I have, myself, inflicted on
Your Most Sacred Heart.
Yet, not enough.
Oh, not enough.
I am so sorry
for every flick of the Lash,
every blow of the Hammer
that I inflicted.
For if You died for my sins,
than I helped to drive in the nails.

YEARNING

If I'm not moving forward then I feel I'm standing still.
Prayer life, a broken record. Vain repetition of prayer?
Knowing there's solid gold,
but I seem to mine it with my fingernails.
Unfilled pockets in the garment of my Soul.
Riches abound, I know but I can't seem to access.
I need to add depth to this spiritual life mine.
We need to be humble before God can use us.
You, God are all, in all, of all.
A finite mind cannot understand infinite, I know.
Yet I know there is more, that I can be more,
learn more, understand more.
The Good, the True, the Beautiful is what I long for.
I long to be in Your presence.
I know that my life doesn't belong only to me.
I belong to God and ultimately that is my Purpose
and that is why I yearn for You.

ANGEL ON MY SHOULDER

When I turn my eyes to God,
there are helpers in the way.
We each have a path, a journey,
Guardian Angels help us not stray.

Assigned to watch over me,
to keep me on my path.
To help me watch my temper.
To overcome my wrath.

The Holy Spirit is withinme,
as important as my heart.
To make sure I don't stumble
or away from God I depart.

We can grieve the Holy Spirit.
He lives within and by our side.
Our bodies are the temple
wherein he does reside.

Be careful where you take Him.
You don't want Him to go away.
If you take Him to sin-filled dungeons,
He'll leave, He will not stay.

Careful! Don't ignore Him.
He'll direct you on your way.
Enjoying the Father's approval
as we go through our day.

THE ONLY WAY

Dear Lord, My Saviour,
as I contemplate and meditate
upon what you did for me, for us,
I am at a loss as how to express to you my thanks.
Words are as good as useless.
My emotions can't seem
to be expressed in any cogent way.
In my mind, I retrace your steps on the way
to Calvary.
I am overcome.

I have finally come to the conclusion
that the only way to thank you is by
Obedience and Worship
totally and faithfully
from my heart
to yours.

I Love You.

WAY OF THE PILGRIM

Regret binds me,
yet the shackles
lay at my feet.

Your Word tells me
that my sins are forgiven
and thrown as far as
the East is from the West.

You've broken my chains
so I might come
closer to You.

Yet, allow a little Regret
to remind me, Lord
that I cannot be self-righteous
for I, too have fallen short.

I have no right to judge others.

Scripture speaks:
Psalm 103:11

"For as high as the heavens are above the earth
so great is His love for those who fear him;
as far as the east is from the west,
so far has He removed our transgressions from us."

SIT'N AND ROCK'N

I'd like to sit on a porch,
in a rocker
and talk to Jesus.
I know some answers,
but pitifully few
Thank you for your teaching,
and your Presence in my life.
But
how do others cope
without you in terror or strife,
illness, hunger and war?
How can they go through
each and every day
with only themselves to rely on?

BUT I DO HAVE A SENSE OF HUMOR

I have a complex case if claustrophobia.

I have a fear of being in small, confined places
and
I have a fear of having a small confined mind.
And
I fear being in a small, confined place
with a crowd of small, confined minds.

PERSONAL GUIDELINES

I have a personal rule regarding Ministries in the Church:

(which I find very effective and freeing-for me)

If I don't like the way someone is doing something,

unless I am willing to take over and do the job myself,

then I don't have a right to complain.

BORING!

Sometimes,
I think
some parts of my life
can be explained
by the word
"ETC!"

HOW CAN I NOT BE JOYFUL?

Than you dearest Jesus
just for being You.
You are found among the many.
You are found among the few.

Each lesson learned
brings You closer to me.
Reading the Scriptures
brings me closer to Thee.

How can I not
hear Your music of Life?
I take Your wisdom
and keep from petty strife.

How can I not be joyful
as I hear Your sacred song
Loving You is the answer.
With You is where I belong.

IT'S PROFOUND

Oh Lord, my God,
You reside within
where I've been forgiven
and freed from Sin.

Far as East to West
my Sin has been flung.*
Your Holy Spirit is in me
and helps me guard my tongue.

You've made my journey
exciting and free.
You teach me and guide me,
You've answered my plea.

How can I thank you?
Nothing can suffice.
You've given me Faith;
a "pearl Beyond Price."

Yes, it's Profound.

Scripture speaks:
*Psalm 103:12 as far as the east is from the west, so far has He removed our transgressions from us.

IT IS SUFFICIENT

Thank you, Lord
for my bed.
I pray for those who have no place
to rest their weary head.

I thank you, God
for my home.
You and I live here,
I'm never alone.

I thank you, Lord
for my garden.
May I pray for the poor;
my heart never harden.

I thank you, Lord
for Bob and Bill in my life.
It was so wonderful
to be their wife.

I thank you, Lord
You're always by my side.
From troubles and fear
I need never hide.

For you are always,
always with me
You guard and guide me,
my life has been set free.

Free from doubt and all fear
that in You I can hide.
That You would be near,
Always by my side.

AT LEAST, I DON'T THINK I AM

I know I'm not stupid
and I don't live in a cave.

But, it's really taken me a long time
to understand that:

I'M NOT IN CHARGE OF
HOW OTHER PEOPLE
ARE SUPPOSED TO BEHAVE!

GETTING OLDER

It doesn't feel good
and it ain't great
to watch your body
deteriorate!

Wrinkles slithering up
and down your skin.
This can't be me;
whose body am I in?

I've been compact,
sleet and thin.
Now my skin looks like mayonnaise
oozing down my chin.

Poets tell us,
but they don't say why:
"If you don't laugh,
you're gonna cry."

Looking sideways …
Oh my, Oh ick!
I can't believe
I look so thick.

Someone told me,
(Oh, what nerve!)
that as we age
we get the face we deserve!

They're not wrinkles.
They're character lines!
I'd better quit.
I'm running out of rhymes.

REALITY

MIDDLE AGE is wonderful.
Now, rather than agonize because
I don't have beautiful legs,
I am so grateful I have two of them
and they both work!

MY
FAVORITES

WHAT IS MORE BEAUTIFUL THAN THIS?

I have found the answer.
I always pause and stare.
It always stops, yet moves me.
It's a man on his knees in prayer.

IN THE BEGINNING

Isn't it strange
that we are here
after Creation's
startling blast?

Before this,
there was no time or space.
There was no future
and no past.

Time and Space
were not needed
God was and is complete.

He thought a thought,
smiled a smile
and stood from
His heavenly throne.

My Son, He said,
You know my heart
Speak it all into
Creation.

The Word was with God.
The Word was God
and brought forth the Creation
of the Father's Holy Word.

John 1:1-5
In the beginning was the Word, and the Word was with God, and the Word was God.

He was with God in the beginning. Through him all things were made; without him nothing was made that has been made. In him was life, and that life was the light of men. The light shines in the darkness, but the darkness has not understood it.

ALL THAT YOU ARE AND ALL THAT YOU WANT TO BE

Have you reached as high as you can?
Have you helped your fellow-man?

Have you soothed an angry heart?
In difficult times do you do your part?

Have you offered the thirsty a cup?
When they fell did you pick them up?

Have you been the person He wants you to be?
Those blind with ambition, have you helped them to see?

Have you defused anger and wrath?
Have you modeled a different path?

Have you reached the suffering as you should?
Have you lifted others when you could?

Did you see the hungry-(they are in Jesus' heart.)
Did you play a life-changing part?

Have you trusted His guidance when it was hard to see?
Have you become the You were meant to be?

AMONG THEM ...

Father God, when I'm among Christians of differing churches, *please* take away the temptation to think:

"I worship God better than they do."

May I show respect and encouragement for their Christian life and help them be the best Christian they can be.

Our proselytizing should be by example, more than confrontation.

Help me to remember that it is the Holy Spirit who is in charge of each of our spiritual lives.

Jesus is the vine, we are the branches. Help me remember that: *Branches don't always grow in the same direction.*

I need to remember that the *Holy Spirit* will lead us on the path He has chosen for us. And if I think someone should, instead, be where I want them to be, then I'm making the assumption the Holy Spirit has made a mistake.

And help me remember this, my Triune God: The Father, Son and Holy Spirit is perfect in all things and in all ways.

Each of us is called in Spirit and in Truth by our personal relationship with God.

May we each walk earnestly and faithfully on the path God has put before us.

I trust the Holy Spirit to lead me (and others) in paths of righteousness.

Discussion is okay, Confrontation is NOT. Confrontation is a game-changer. It causes walls to be raised immediately.

We can be strong in conviction, but again, "a soft answer turneth away truth"*

Strong conviction is often more forceful when delivered in a soft voice.

Dialogue, not Confrontation.

We are called above all, to act and react with LOVE, because GOD is LOVE.

When I see someone on a path leading in an obviously wrong and/or dangerous direction, I must use reasoning, pointing out any dangers, clarifying, show them, help them to see and help me to remember that: ***The greatest weapon I have is prayer.*** It's one of the greatest weapons of all and also use recourse to the Holy Spirit. Ask the Holy Spirit into the situation. Powerful things happen when He is involved.

Remember Paul, whom God chastised because he used fear and violence to bring souls to Him. Sometimes a warrior needs to know which weapons to use. Who can withstand the power of the Holy Spirit and Prayer?

As the Sun shines for us all, let us *all* rest and remain in the Light of the Son.

1 Peter 3:15
But in your hearts set apart Christ as Lord. Always be prepared to give an answer to everyone who asks you to give the reason for the hope that you have. But do this with gentleness and respect.

Proverbs 15:1
A gentle answer turns away wrath, but a harsh word stirs up anger.

INTROSPECTION INTERRUPTED BY REALITY

Shadows sweeping across the room,
like a mystical, ethereal broom.
Light and Darkness subtly play
a game of light and dark and grey.

Sunlight playing hide and seek.
I may sit here for a week.
Alone-ness now presents as gift
So many thoughts my mind does sift.

Sadness and Joy reflected there,
-and here, again there and everywhere!
Is it death that stalks the room?
Or merely a cloud covering
the moon?

Such a quixotic, quiet night,
my heart is heavy, yet it's light.
I'm embraced by being alone.
Oh no! Oh noooo! There goes the phone!

UNFULFILLED

How many are living
with broken dreams,
unfulfilled schemes that grew
in youthful minds and hearts.

Aspirations slowly fade
from a dreamer's plan
as youth becomes a man and
responsibilities demand practicality.

Where did these dreams go?
How did they leave?
Did the loss cause us to grieve?
Or did they slowly fade?

As time flies by
life demands we adjust.
It's a practical must
that we face reality.

Looking back in fading years,
finding small dreams get replaced,
big dreams get displaced and
we find ourselves in someone else's life

(So many dreams are gone)

ONLY THROUGH YOU

Only through You
can we be strong.
We try to do right
but sometimes we're wrong.

"They know not what they do"
is what You said.
Sometimes breathing people
are spiritually dead.

Watch the way
they treat each other.
Not knowing that others
are their sister, their brother.

They stumble through life
ignoring your Throne.
They couldn't care less
that You remain unknown.

They plod along
accepting Satan's curse.
They are unaware, don't care
Eternal Life has entered the Universe.

WONDER IF THEY HAVE A WELCOME WAGON

There is a place called SADNESS.
It's dark and gloomy
and its people never smile.

HOPELESS, a neighbor
stops by too often to chat for awhile.

The town's plaza's named ISOLATION.
The social life centers there.

Their police force is DEPRESSION
and it monitors how they care.

The population is burdened
by the backpack of its' worries and its' strife.

Sometimes LIFE seems a near-death experience.

PATTERNS

When all around seems so very wrong.
Life not gentled by poem or song.

All around are asking "Why?"
Seems tears must follow every sigh.

God allowing such a thing!
Dirges played; no one can sing.

We are called to place our trust,
completely believing He is just.

The bigger picture we don't see.
Life is like a tapestry.

Threads all over hanging free.
No pattern can we seem to see.

When at last it's turned around,
we'll see its' pattern; its' purpose found.

From birth to death He wove it all.
Our life has meaning after all.

PUTTING IN THE STITCHES THAT HOLD ME TOGETHER

Love is the invisible
fabric of our lives,
woven with golden threads
of contentment,
silver threads
of security
and
of course,
brass buttons
so you can survive.

NO LOVE, NO LIFE

Lonely old house
sitting on a hill.
Empty rooms;
no laughter, it's still.

No children to run
out and in.
No smiles, no fun.
No jokes, no grins.

Silence is heavy
upon the air.
Who could know
that a house could care?

Empty rooms,
no love, no life.
No murmuring echoes
from love, from life.

Who could know
what a heart can bear?
A house is not a home,
unless love is there.

MY TWILIGHT

SWIFTLY MOVES THE YEARS

My time is winding now.
I hear it's gentle tick-tock.
Not fainter, not slower
yet I am becoming aware
now of that gentle sound.

It's not minutes that I now grab onto,
but
life affirming moments that I now grasp.

Time spent with loved ones.
Hugs and kisses from family.
Awareness of who really loves you.
Quiet times with friends
with their laughter
ringing through the room..
A good book.
The smell of Spring.

The feel of a baby as she snuggles in.
New Life:
Creations Crown
reminding old arms of when they, too, were young
and held their own babies.
Holding a babe is never forgotten.
Arms ache for it
and memory replays its' Song.

FINISH

I'm afraid that
I'll be on my death bed,
looking up at someone
and say:
"I never had much fun,
but I was SO responsible!"

Last hours: DAY IS DRAWING NIGH

No clocks exist for me because no time remains.
I am at the pinnacle of my life,
the place where no time exists because
I have used all that was allotted me.
I know that a special moment has come
to account for the time I sent here on earth.
That portion if time in eternity that I was given
to learn and grow in love and knowledge of
My God, My Saviour.
How have I used the time He bought for me?
Accounting for my life, this meditative time is all that is now left to me.
Have I learned all the many lessons we are to learn?
Loving kindness, service to others, joy.
Loving our neighbors as much as ourselves.
To be honorable, of integrity, aware of my Soul.
Loving God with my whole heart, my whole Soul.
And yes, I have learned that I am called to deal with:
those who gossip, are mean-spirited, and judgmental as well as
to love our enemies and to pray for them! (Yes!)
Have I overcome the lessons of my childhood
and learned my lessons well, Lord?
Is my name in the Book?
And last (and I feel foolish asking)
am I a sheep or a goat?
You are the Good Shepard, will I hear Your call?

-continuted-

page 2 Last hours: DAY IS DRAWING NIGH

Scripture Speaks:

Matthew 25:32
All the nations will be gathered before Him and He will separate the people one from another as a shepherd separates the sheep from the goats. He will put the sheep on His right and the goats on His left.

25:34 Then the King will say to those on his right, "Come you who are blessed by my Father, take your inheritance, the kingdom prepared for you since the creation of the world."

25:41 Then He will say to those on His left: Depart from me you who are cursed, into the eternal fire prepared for the devil and his angels.

Psalm 69:28 May they be blotted out of the book of life and not be listed with the righteous.

“TILL WE MEET AGAIN

I crossed the divide on an Angel’s wing!
Can you imagine such a wonderful thing?
Do not cry or weep for me.
I’m now a Soul-completely free!
I’ll get to see Jesus face to face;
look at His wonders, understand His Grace.
Once again in the arms of those I had loved.
(They all were waiting as I rose above.)
I can look down, all you I can see.
Your laughter, your love meant the world to me.
Thank you for all the joy you gave me.
Do all you can do, be all you can be.
I’m in God’s presence, can you relate?
How important is love, how destructive is hate.
Jesus stands beside me and takes my hand.
We reviewed my life, now I understand:
-Sorrow and suffering, good and the bad.
-Lessons I learned, understanding to be had.
-Love to receive and to give.
-My character to build, a life to live.
We reviewed my life, He discussed it with me.
How gentle, how loving and wise is He.
“I’ve prepared you a mansion” is what He said.
I’m living more fully now that I’m dead.

Scripture speaks:
PPP
John 14:2
Do not let your hearts be troubled. Trust in God, trust also in Me. In my Father’s house are many rooms; if it were not so, I would have told you. I am going to prepare a place for you. I will come back and take you to be with me that you also may be where I am. You know the way to the place where I am going.

YOUR PURPOSE OR STANDING AT THE GATES

Will you have the answer?
What will you say?
Did you live fully
in all you did each day?

Now, about that time I gave to you.
Did you learn all you could?
Did you learn about me?
Didn't you think you should?

I waited patiently.
The Spirit gave you each a sign,
You may not believe it.
But your Heart and Soul are Mine.

OH, SO IMPORTANT!

Live your Life so that
the last words you say
aren't an apology.

HE AND I

EUREKA!*

I want to walk on the Path of Light.
The Light of Knowledge, Wisdom and Joy.
Walking toward an Ever brighter and Heart-Filling life.

I want to walk on the path of Faith.
Joy and Peace He gives to me
from what he has written on my Heart.

I can Live, Love and Learn
'cuz I walk on this path of Light
I can only give what I allow myself to receive.
I must shelter my mind from evil and negativity.

With open Mind and open Heart.
I give to You as He gives to me.
I have found the Secret of Life.

He is my Light, my Forever.

*Eureka means- I have found it!

PLEASE

Lord, give me
eyes that see
their purpose here.

Ears that hear
Your call.

Lips that speak
of Praise in Prayer.

A heart that first
fills with Love for You,
overflowing,
and then reaches out
to all Your children.

SET APART

The Bible tells us
that the followers of Christ
"are in this world,
but we are not <u>of</u> this world."

As I get older, I understand this
more and more.
There is this sensation, at times,
of being in a box within a box.

Quite frankly, it's oddly comforting.
It seems to enable me to sit back
and discern and really see
what is going on in this world around me.

COMMUNION

A coming together
of You and me and Jesus.
A moment in time
that happens so quickly
that real meaning can
be snatched away from me
in thoughtless musings.
I want to be totally with You, in You,
and aware of this enormous Gift of Love.
I ponder and store up how I want to receive You:
with Reverence,
with Focus,
with Joy,
with Humility
with Awareness,
and with great Thanksgiving.
A giving-over of my total self to You.
How quickly my mind can let this determination fade.
I want to be totally with You, in You;
aware of this great act of Love.

That He paid the price for me, (for ME!) that I might gain eternal life and be in the presence of God and receive Godly Love for eternity.

Greater Love hath this than no man,
That he give up his life for another.

John 10:11, 15, 17
Mark 10:24
John 15:5

MY HEART, MY SOUL

I open the door
into my heart
and there,
once again,
I find You.
A peace.
Peace I find there.
A satisfaction
that I am where
I'm meant to be.
The stress of the world
does not come
into this place.
A sanctuary
in this Sanctuary.
The world cannot
rage against me here.

COME TO ME

Come to me, my children.
Walk and talk with me
I gave you My substance
as I hung upon that tree.

I gave my all and suffered
to overcome your sin
I hung bloody, tho' not defeated,
salvation could begin.

I'm in your heart and soul.
I have called you each by name.
You are called to be my child
you'll never be the same.

YOUR MANY FACES

Come to me fisherman, fisher of men.
Walk across the water.

Oh come to me story man, man of stories.
Tell me a parable to teach me life's lessons.

Oh, come to me miracle man, man of miracles.
Turn the water into wine and heal the blind and lame.

Oh come to me humble man, man of humility.
You let John baptize You, even tho' You are the son of God.

Oh come to me salvation man, man of salvation.
You paid the price for me to see the Father for eternity.

Oh, come to me Holy One, Holy One.
I need You in my life.

SEEMINGLY ALONE

Oh, Lord I am so afraid
and you seem so far away.
Yet Your Word has told me
in Your heart I'll stay.

Yet, I cannot touch You;
nor look into Your face.
So I am very thankful
for Your Gift of Grace.

You whisper Your great wisdom
into my mind and soul.
I keep growing and learning
but I long for you so.

Time flies by so quickly
and yet can seem so long
until I'll be with You.
Hope lingers long.

MY NEW LIFE

Lord, we need You in this place.
Your Wisdom, Your Love, Your Grace.
I will worship, give praise to You.
I'll follow and thank You in all that I do

You bring me Joy, my soul You will keep.
My thankfulness so big, it causes me to weep.
We can only define You in human terms.
We struggle, we ponder, our pathway is firm.

The mind of God, the hands of God, the wrath.
You've placed me on my special path.
It's a very physical and active love.
Tho' the Spirit is often revealed as a dove.

We clap our hands and jump for joy
when faced with reality of Mary's little boy.
Our worries and cares we release,
for now we have You and can rest in Your peace.

The Angels lift in song their heavenly voices.
He is a God of Love, He rejoices.

COMMUNION, THE EUCHARIST

That you come to me!
The Great I Am.
Father of All.
Name above all names.
Creator of the Universe.
Blessed Redeemer.
Living Word.
The one, true God.
You are the Light of the World,
who leads me out of the Darkness.
That you come to me!
Bread of Life.
You feed me to sustain my Spiritual Life.
All you ask in return
in Acknowledgement of Your Divinity,
an obedient Spirit,
a willing Heart.
You gave me a Soul
so that my Life has a higher purpose.
That you come to me!
You always are waiting, watching for a Soul
to realize its' Source,
to make its' life-altering commitment
To Goodness, Mercy, to Love, to Worship
the one, true God.
You caution: Remain vigilant and beware of neglect
of your Spiritual Life.
In appearance of bread and wine, Body and Blood
You come to me!
Your Heart always hears my cries of sorrow, of despair
and my shouts, exultations and songs of joy
worshipping only You.

LOVE LETTER TO JESUS

You are my Soul's definition
without words.

You are the horizon,
I sense no beginning and no end.

You are the clouds,
beautiful and ever-changing.

You are the mountains,
drawing my eyes and thoughts ever upward.

I GET A GLIMPSE

You are the Sun.
You are the Moon.
You seem to tarry,
yet You whisper "soon".
You are the Right,
yet we see such Wrong.
Tho' we differ so greatly
we know You're right all along.
To some you say "Stay',
to some You say "Go".
To some You say, "Fast",
To others "Go Slow".
I've never seen you,
yet I know You.
With Faith I accept,
and know what to do.
You reach out to claim me,
but my acceptance is slow.
Yet, somehow,
I always know,
that I know,
that I know.

I COME TO YOU

I come to you, Lord, with a heart filled with knowledge
and thankfulness that comes from Your teaching.

I come to You, Lord with a heart filled with Love.

I come to you, Lord, with a mind filled with yearning
to know more about You and longing to grow steadfastly.

I come to You, Lord, with eyes that see and are aware
of the blessings all around me that You seem to pour
into my life.

I come to you, Lord, with a mind that, at times,
stills and is aware of Your teaching, Your instruction.

I come to You, Lord, with ears that hear Your voice
and am learning to discern Your teaching.

But, doesn't it seem, Lord,
that the most important first step is that:
I come You?

For the Year of Mercy – 2016

YOUR MERCY

That You should accept my Praise is a Mercy to me.
That You should even hear my prayers is a great Mercy to me.
We merit nothing and yet You engage with us.
Has Your Love and Mercy no bounds?
You listen to us even when
we're not even worthy of Your attention.
How great is Your love.
I cannot be holy, for only One is holy.
I can only be obedient.
I can only be in Your will.
You raise me up not because I am deserving
But because You are Great Love.
My Soul is filled with delight because
of Your great Mercy.
Nothing have I done to merit this but receive
only through Your great Mercy and Love.
Truly You are my Saviour

I WANT TO GROW!

My Spirit seems so tiny, Lord.
So little.
I want to spend my waking hours
in Thanksgiving, in Joy.
I come near to grasping it, Lord,
and then it fades.
Where is my stamina of Faith?
I want to be a Giant for you:
praising, giving thanks and joyful
in my every waking moment.
Please smooth and widen my path
so I may quicken my steps
on my spiritual journey.
Until my Soul is open and complete,
until I can "see" you
nodding and smiling in approval.

AGAPE LOVE

(Agape-unselfish, unconditional love)

Nearly 40 years ago when I first learned about God's agape love I was Thrilled to be introduced to this concept. Much later I heard it described in this manner:

The Sun shines on the flower and the manure pile
in the same manner and intensity.
Not because one is more deserving than the other,
but because it is the Sun's nature to shine.

I was thrilled to understand that God loved me not because I was deserving but because it is God's nature to love in this bounteous way. This is who He is.

I would never be deserving of this love, would never be good enough and yet there was this knowledge, this hope that I was not lost to Him.

Scripture speaks:

1 John 4:8 … God is Love.

US

GIFT FOR A FRIEND

May you never lose your Wonder
as you increase in Wisdom.
Nor lose your Laughter
as you face the realities of Life.
May your Faith grow
as will your Joy.
May Gratefulness hold hands with you
and
May the Beauty around you
imprint on your Soul.
and
May your love of God
color each moment
of your life.
and
May you dwell
in the house of the Lord
forever and ever.

MOMENTS

Come, sit by me
and we will enjoy
the silence together.
Hold my hand
so I may feel our connection.
Let me see the reflection
of the sunset in your eyes.
Know that you are
my companion.
I will always be
by your side
Come, sit by me
And absorb our togetherness.

TOGETHER

Pray for one another.
Life is challenging, hard for everyone.
We have so many lessons to learn
and some of those lessons cause us
to climb mountains and traverse chasms.
So lift each other up. Encourage each other.
Be there for each other.
The help and love you give away does not diminish you.
In some strange way, it makes you stand taller.
When you give of yourself, it makes you a bigger person.
As you walk through life, you carry the knowledge
that you try to be a Good Person, a child of God.
On those spiritually cloudy days
this will be a light that will shine inside you
If we all helped each other, lifted each other up
what a world it could be, would be!
Kindness and Encouragement to others
helps your Soul to grow
and
it's pleasing to God.

Win-win!

"FOOL RUSH IN WHERE ANGELS FEAR TO TRED"

We are slowly taking over the prerogatives of God.
Who should be born.
Who should die (and why).
Thinking we are in charge.
That we can solve all problems.
That with cloning, we can create life.
That we can change the face of the earth without consequence.
And when the seas roar,
when tidal waves cause astonishing destruction,
the very air and wind spin everything in its'path into annihilation,
the earth jolts, trembles and leaps in protest of what we do,
we watch all this with mouths open and hearts closed.
We still do not acknowledge the power of God.

We *still* do not see our arrogance.

for Chauncey

HEARTBREAK

I couldn't touch you baby boy.
Couldn't allow myself that joy.
I knew the pain that faced my heart
when I said goodbye, for we had to part.

My life, so confused and afraid was I.
I knew if I held you, my heart would die
I had to give you a better life.
But the pain, oh the pain cut like a knife.

Though many and sundry I could blame.
I would never hear you call my name.
For to you, I'd not be Mom, my dear.
I couldn't take care of you; it was clear.

You never were a mistake, my son.
Some things we do, can't be undone.
In my heart you'll always be;
always be a part of me.

I wouldn't see you learn to walk, to run.
But you were my first, my baby, my son.
Though for many years we were apart,
you were always in my heart.

A GIFT OF LOVE

I'm so thankful to the woman
who gave me my son.
I know this wasn't easy
for her to have done.

A sacrifice she made for him.
She thought only of her son.
"Please give him your love and care,
for he's a special one."

What a sacrifice she made,
to give her babe to me.
What an act of love for him.
I can understand, I see.

Her Mother's love wanted the best for him
and she could not provide.
So she put him in my heart, my arms.
Her arms empty, she grieved and cried.

You were her loss
and my gain.
I understood and was aware
of her tremendous pain.

HAPPY LITTLE BOY

I've got two Mothers
What a lucky guy!
I love to dance and laugh and sing
and hold my hands up high.

I've got two Mothers.
God loves me so, so much.
He says I have a loving heart,
'cuz I've been loved a bunch.

God said "This boy is special.
Look how he laughs and sings.
Look how much He loves me.
I might give him two of everything!"

"I'll not make him perfect.
I'll give him a few flaws.
For in his weakness, I am strength.
He bows down to My laws"

"He knows I am his God.
He's accepted my Holy Son.
He listens to the Holy Spirit.
When I call my Saints, he'll be one."

Chauncey:
You weren't abandoned.
You were relocated!

GOODBYE MOM

You'll never forget her.
Nor would you ever want to.
But how much richer is your entire life
because God put you two together.
How much poorer your life would have been
if she had never touched your life.

Your birth-mother
made sure that
you were given every chance.
A mother and a father.

She wanted the best for you.
And you certainly got it!

Amen? Amen!

THE LAW

THE LAW

This section to be written about the negative, the heart breaking side of law enforcement. That's because it has been written by the widow of two brave men who protected and served.

I would venture to say that most of those in Law Enforcement love this job and are proud of what they do.

But since "those who sit and wait also serve" we worry, we wait and have compassion for the difficult times:

He called me almost yelling "where are the boys, where are the boys?" who were pre-schoolers. His job as that time was to photograph crime scenes and they had found the bodies of three pre-schoolers who got trapped in an abandoned refrigerator and suffocated when the door swung shut as they were playing inside. And he had to take photos of their little bodies.

Me, in an emergency room, waiting for a friend who needed attention: (Two sheriff deputies talking) "I was there last night on a domestic disturbance call and I told her she must leave this situation. (But she, as victims often do, stayed) I was called again today and he had thrown her off the balcony of their house."

He came home and said-"they threw rocks at us last night" I only said 'Oh?" Thinking it was gravel. Reading the paper the next day, the words "large chunks of concrete' caught my eye. When I confronted him he just smiled at me.

He told me the story of a motorcycle officer who went down and sustained a compound fracture of the leg. The neighbors, gathered around him and began applauding.

The many other stories that caused me to tell my friends "I think I know what human beings are capable of more than you but I will never tell you the stories because you won't want to have them in your mind,-you won't be able to fully forget them.

I remember watching tv in our den with a neighbor. It was 10pm and there was a knock at the front door. I almost stopped breathing-thinking no one comes to your door this late at night. But they wouldn't call you by phone to make a notification if he'd been wounded or killed. (I was blessedly relieved to find out it was my Neighbor's boyfriend who was looking for her.)

And I realized that this fear is always in the back of your mind. The fear, large or small is always there. The possibility is always there.

My stepson, a Sergeant with the Sheriff's dept was at the scene of a man barricaded in his home with an arsenal of guns. A deputy was shot and they moved a car in and brought him back to the medical personnel. They told my step-son-get his holster off, get his holster off! He straddled his fellow-deputy and was frantically removing the holster. Then he happened to look up and the deputy's face was gone.

And if these are the stories that I am willing to share, you can imagine what other incidents I feel I can't tell you (Well ... no, you can't.)

CIVILIAN SOLDIER

A Civilian soldier
prowls the streets.
Ever watchful,
he patrols his "beat"

Low level combat
and watchful eyes,
ride the streets
and watch over our lives.

We pay no attention
to a stranger.
Trusting and naïve,
unaware of danger.

They stand against evil,
facing the twisted and mad.
Strangely moved by good,
they see mostly bad.

Saving children,
they fight the drugs
that destroy generations
by mindless things.

They stand as brothers
in this war.
To Protect And Serve
is the oath they swore.

In service TO the community
Invested IN the community

COWBOYS IN SQUAD CARS

Tiny, little cowboy boots.
They look so sweet.
Size 3 and ½,
usually on the wrong feet.

Red felt cowboy hat.
The horse is a scooter.
Soft, plastic gun-belt
and tiny six shooter.

Grade school Saturdays:
Cowboys, Indians, even F.B.I.
Take turns being good and bad.
If you fall, you must not cry.

The cowboy hats and boots are gone.
Years ticking on life's clock.
Gun-belt now of leather.
Toy gun replaced by Glock.

Memories touchingly innocent.
You look back upon those days.
Reality can be painful now,
watching as society frays.

IN SERVICE

With gun, baton, pepper spray and taser,
you tune into coded violence.
Non-inflected voices roll on as if it were an epic poem,
reporting chaos in all its forms.

Lights and sirens blaring, adrenaline pounding.
Keep your own reactions locked down!
Minds reviewing procedures and directions.
Speed of vehicle matching heartbeat.

Gladiators of the street,
you have become "The Thin Blue Line"
and stand between us and violence
in all its sick, degraded forms.

Finding that good people
can do bad things,
but there are those few
who are just truly evil.

You see the precious gift of life
rotted into drug infused days
and nights of torment
and families fragmenting.

Doing what you can.
You can only do what you can do.
The conundrum is how do you know all you know
and keep your personal life in balance?

UNDER THEIR WINGS

And they walk among us with the truncheon of truth
and love for the law in their hearts.
Heartbreak is their some-time companion
as they go from day to day.

They stand between us and evil
so we may stay in the land of the free
and home of the brave.
We have no idea what it costs.

We rest in our homes,
kiss loved ones goodnight
and expect to wake up in the morning.
Unaware that a price has been paid.

While they ride through the nights,
watching, waiting, listening.
To guard us, to make sure
that our sleep, our lives stay unbroken.

They serve with little recognition.
But they believe in the Law.
Of Right overcoming Wrong.
Good over Evil.

Joy comes from
keeping their city safe.
Of taking predators off the streets.
They are the guardians of our cities.

And sometimes,
Justice peeks out
from under the blindfold
and sees the cost.

THE SHUFFLING BEAT OF THE PRISONER'S FEET

Through courtyard grey,
prisoners' shuffling feet,
coming forward
their fate to meet.

Watch your back.
Play the "Bad Dude" card.
You're never safe
in a prison yard.

To fear your brother,
or the Guard;
the accepted violence
of a prison yard.

Day, as night,
ever grey and cold.
Darkness fills your mind
as you grow old.

A life ordained
by drugs, knife or gun.
You can't undo
what you have done.

No opening seen
in soul or life.
Seeing nothing better
for themselves but strife.

How few escape
to a better place.
Thought better to die
Than to lose face.

With heart so sold,
yet rage is hot.
Compassion does die
and begins to rot.

Choices made,
Lives filled with dross.
Wretched pain
and endless loss.

Family incantations,
Your failings they tell.
Society turns its back
And condemns you as well.

COPS

A weary pity sometimes acts as a second skin
and sometimes you feel it accompany
your interactions with the public.
Mountains of paperwork.
Stretches of unbelievable boredom.
Then, suddenly Adrenaline!
Heart stopping moments of danger.
Quick seconds in which to make Life and Death decisions.
At times your life depends on instants and inches.
Picking up pieces of peoples lives
and again the weary pity covers you.
Trying not to agonize over the children.
Those who are beaten, neglected, unfed
unclean, given drugs, forced into licentiousness.
The horrendous abuse.
Tho' you try, you can't forget the children.
Yet, you persevere knowing that some
of Societies broken ones will walk free,
that the system sometimes fails.
And on you go, day after day, night after night
because the perfect center of you
believes in Law, in Justice.
The power of Good overcoming Evil.
At times you can almost believe that
Civilization has a chance to advance.

WOUNDED BUT UNSEEN

He's good at his job,
but he walks with pain.
Pain in his eyes and in his heart.
The knowledge of the depravity of man
and what they are capable of becoming and doing
is a burden too heavy for his shoulders to carry and longer:
The badge and the gun come with a veneer of Macho.
How can he admit to this pain?
The boyish pranks and the gallows humor
no longer hold the stark knowledge at bay.
The children, OH the children!
He feels that he committed to protect them
but is not always able.
Heavy, heavy is the heart that patrols a beat.

SPIRITUAL
LIFE

WE ARE YOURS

Now, for awhile,
we are sojourners in a far land.
You have placed within us a Guide
to show us the path we must walk upon
to find our way to You.
This Guide accompanied
by our hearts, so in love with You,
and
our obedience
will bring us to the foot of Your throne.

And there we will be Your people
and You will be our God.

Scripture speaks:

LEV 26:12
I will walk among you and be your God and you will be my people.

HOLY SPIRIT

Be the guardian
of my Soul.

The watchman over
my words.

The gate that guards
against unloving actions.

And when I whisper
Your name,
you clear my mind
of unworthy thoughts.

LORD, HOLY SPIRIT, FATHER GOD

Help us to remember that the only way to show You we are grateful is
through Obedience,
through Worship,
Thankfulness
& Loving Each Other.

Loving when people sometimes seem, or actually are, unlovable.

Jesus, our Saviour, we are grateful for Your immense sacrifice
so we may spend eternity with our triune God.

We are a broken people, Lord and sometimes I wonder
if we aren't allowed to be broken so that we rely on You
to put the pieces together again with
the glue of Wisdom and the cord of Infinite Love
with our acknowledgement that each painful step
brings us closer to You.

Through any and all difficulties
may we always turn to You,
the Light of the World,
rejecting the darkness
realizing that we are Your child
and
You will never forsake us.

We must refuse to be separated from You.

We lift hands and hearts to Jesus, our Saviour.

Scripture speaks:

2CO 6:7-10
In truthful speech and in the power of God; with weapons of righteousness in the right hand and in the left, through glory and dishonor, bad report and good report, genuine, yet regarded as impostors, known, yet regarded as unknown, dying and yet we live on; beaten and yet not killed, sorrowful, yet always rejoicing, poor, yet making many rich, having nothing and yet possessing everything.

DIRECTION

Scene: A wedding
Location: the town of CANA

In five words.
In 5 words!

Mary, as she pointed to Jesus and said to the wine steward:

"DO WHATEVER HE TELLS YOU."

Yes,
yes,
yes!

"DO WHATEVER HE TELLS YOU!"

The best, the most true, wisest words ever spoken.

In five words she summarizes it all!

AMAZING!

The answer to the purpose and direction of our life.

Scripture speaks:
At the wedding at Cana-His first miracle.
John 2:5
His mother said to the servants, "Do whatever He tells you."
John 2:11
This turning of water into wine was the first of His miraculous signs, Jesus performed in Cana of Galilee. He thus revealed His glory and His disciples put their faith in Him.

WHO, WHAT, WHERE

Why are we here? What is our purpose?
We hunt for answers
to assuage our fears,
our incomprehension.

Purpose, you say?
A reason to live.
The truth, the light, the way
leads our way to meaning.

By instinct, we look up.
Somehow we know
the Chalice, the Cup
is our pathway.

MAKE ROOM!

Everything in us - - - - -
every thought,
every word,
every action,
every breath
must reach out.
Away from self,
so God can find space
to come in
and be part of us.

JESUS IS THE SHEPHERD, WE ARE THE SHEEP

To those of us who think we're so wise, so learned, so all-knowing, so important, that what we want is so important, that what we do is so important, that we are so important.

Consider this:
He chooses the foolish to confound the wise.

He chose the symbol of the Shepherd for His son. For the Shepherd looks after His sheep. Being a Shepherd in that time and place was one of the most lowly jobs. A job with the least prestige possible and on the lowest rung of society's standard.

And, if you learn about sheep, you will discover that sheep are among the most stupid of animals.

Therefore, the inevitable conclusion is that we are not so important, that what we do or want is not so important. That looking down on another person is just laughable. Because we are nothing except who we are in Christ. That all there is to be, to do, to acquire, to accomplish is only what He has given us.

Scripture speaks:

1 CO 1:20 Has not God made foolish the wisdom of the world?
And
1 CO 1:27 But God chose the foolish things of the world to shame the wise.

LEARN OR BURN

We are on a journey.
It was planned that way.
I find it just amazing
what I can learn each day!

Allowing no boredom
or the sophisticates' "ennui",
There's enough to keep us busy
if we would only see.

Each day has a lesson.
A plethora of being aware.
Myraid lessons of understanding:
how to love and how to care.

If God judges us as we judge others,
indeed how do we dare?
Hair raising possibilities
of which we become aware.

RELATIONSHIP

We are Covenant people
and yet we become distorted and broken by Sin.
Did I choose You?
Or is He who is within me guiding my path?
When did my heart, my soul, my mind
open to the realization, the awareness that
I am not unto myself.
I belong to You.
You knew us before Creation.
The Father said, "I knit you in your Mother's womb."

Farther than the wind blows,
higher than the heavens,
wider than the forever horizon
His Love for us stands forever.

Scripture speaks:

EPHESIANS 1:4
For He chose us in him before the creation of the world to be holy and blameless in his sight.

JOHN 15:16
You did not choose me, but I chose you and appointed you to go bear fruit that will last. Then the Father will give you whatever you ask in my name.

DON'T YOU KNOW?

Wordly wisdom is incomplete.
There is a wisdom outside of us:
out, on, around, and through us.
A wisdom of the soul.
Wisdom embedded in our heart, our soul.
A holiness that will teach us, guide us.
Given to us, we are a temple
where the Holy Spirit resides.
Take care not to grieve this Holy Spirit.
In our limited understanding we must learn
that this Wisdom dwells **in** us.
Over and above, it is the among
the most precious things we have.
It guides us through difficulties,
whose purpose we do not understand.

Scripture speaks:

1CO 3:16 Don't you know that you yourselves are God's temple and that God's Spirit lives in you? If anyone destroys God's temple God will destroy him; for God's temple is sacred and you are the temple.

1CO 6:19 Do you not know that your body is a temple of the Holy Spirit, who is in you, whom you have received from God: You are not your own, you were bought at a price. Therefore honor God with your body.

2CO 6:16 What agreement is there between the temple of God and idols? For we are temple of the living God.

SANCTUARY

This is a house of Worship.
Reverence abides within.
Here we come to learn and grow
to rise above our Sin.

Here we come together
to worship our God, our Lord.
Here we come to proclaim
His word, our light and our sword.

Here we come
with Thanksgiving and Joy.
Raising hands and hearts in
Praise to the Son, Mary's little boy.

Here we come with
our Sorrows and Tears
to see His wisdom
and help us handle our fears.

COME TO ME

Come to me, my children.
Walk and talk with me
I gave you My substance
as I hung upon that tree.

I gave my all and suffered
to overcome your sin
I hung bloody, tho' not defeated,
salvation could begin.

I'm in your heart and soul.
I have called you each by name.
You are called to be my child.
You'll never be the same.

EXPAND YOUR VOCABULARY, EXPAND YOUR LIFE

Let us not be like the soldiers at Jesus' crucifixion.
Near enough to touch the suffering, the dying, but no concern.
Insensitive, laughing, joking, gambling for His clothes.
We can't heal all wounds.
We can't end all suffering.
But we can try to do our part.
We can add the words I LOVE YOU to our vocabulary.
We can add GIVING to our actions.
We can add VOLUNTEERING to our lives.
We can REACH OUT and help one another.
Simple KINDNESS and COURTSEY
can be added to our lives.

WINGS OF THE MIND
... OPENING UP TO POSSIBILITIES

That there is
Someone
who created me
There is
Purpose
to my life
There is
a *Difference*
to be made
There is
Life after Death.
There is
Love
There is
Honesty.
There is
Integrity.
There is
Light
to shine upon
the Knowledge
that God loves me.
There is
Gratefulness
that I know that
Jesus died for me.

TRAVEL

NEW ENGLAND IN THE FALL

Pumpkins stealing
their orange color
from autumn leaves
and coming in second best.

Sumac challenging you
to describe its' peculiar red.
None calls it true and it dances
away from you in the sunlight-laughing.

Gentle breezes cascades leaves down,
making a scraping sound
as they reluctantly somersault
and skid across the ground.

Low stone walls
standing three centuries and more
seeing much, saying nothing.
Silent spectators of war, of toil.

Small towns,
small cemeteries, centuries old.
Saddest of all,
small graves here and there.

Lakes, ponds and streams,
a quiet respite from the chorus of color.
Trees reflect and expand in the moment
in the mirror of water.

Nature's fire in a final flare
before withdrawing.
A defiant gesture at the
cold, silent season to come.

THE TROUBLES

I raised my sons for Ireland.
I gave them up to the fight.
Many a time I sat in the dark
through a long and fearful night.

Sean, who was my youngest;
a bright and laughing lad.
The last born was the first to die.
It broke the heart of his Dad.

Nights I cried to Jesus.
Days I walked in pain.
My second born, my Seamus
lay bloodied in the rain.

The green of my land soothes me.
Heather and Gorse are at my hand.
The rain and prayers sustain me.
Oh, how I love this land.

I gave my sons to Ireland.
Each of us did our part.
And then, the war, the terrible war
tore the Shamrock from my heart.

PALM SPRINGS

Place of contradictions.
Oasis and desert
opposite each other,
in space, in purpose,
in beauty, in use.
Colors assaulting you.
Flowering trees, shrubs,
plants and weeds.
The heady fragrance
of the masses of flowers
vying for attention
with strong perfumes
of rich matrons strolling
the shops, the boulevards.
Walkers, cyclers, joggers:
Youth struggled for,
maintained, bought.
Wildflowers mocking
planned, formal landscaping.
Well-tended bodies
mocking old age.

UTAH

The earth
speaks of
Him.
Nature in
balanced perfection.
Majestic
cliffs.
Profound
canyons.
The stillness
of the earth,
until the wind
sings His name.

SYLVAN LAKE-SYLVAN PASS

(East entrance to Yellowstone in Wyoming)

Sylvan sounds of silence.
Silver streams and
Small, smudged patches of snow.
Seemingly out of place
In the warm Summer sun,
Yet owning the patch
On which it lays
With silent authority.
Children playing in the snow
While the sun browns their arms.
Boys and fathers fishing,
Casting into the lake,
While casting glances
Of comradeship and contentment
At each other.
Pines overlooking all
As God's sentinels.
Waterfalls cascading.
Some giving, falling,
While others gleefully leap forth
With gladness of the day.
Eyes drawn up
Mountains of trees
To even higher
Black, barren peaks
Clothed in snow.
Birds flitting,
Diving, Swooping.
Alive with movement.
Flowers alive with color.
Moving only
As the breeze commands.
A fragile whisper
In the face of raw power
Of the beauty all around.

GRAND CANYON

Nature stands as an
irrefutable witness
and fairly shouts a testimony
of His presence.

The work of His hand
from infinitesimal to infinite
silently waiting for us to notice
their existence as proof of I AM.

The unending horizon,
a silent allegory:
'As it was in the beginning
is now and ever shall be."

The Alpha and Omega concept
of Him - - too large to grasp.
Our finite minds groping
for the reality of infinity.

MICHIGAN MORNING

Fog laying sleepily
upon the ground.

Cool air briskly
shaking the trees awake.

Poplar trees shivering
in the early morning dew.

Grey skies grumpily
ignoring the sun.

Crows noisily interrupting
the dawn's shushing pleas for silence.

Green and grey seem the only colors
nature's using from her palette.

A quiet time
for quiet thoughts.

TIBURON

(Northern California)

Sailboats gliding
on unseen feet
across the shimmering
upside-down sky.

Skyline viewed across the Bay.
Buildings tumbling together
as if there must be
unseen elbows pushing for space.

Rocky shores welcome commuters,
placed in uniforms by conformity.
Flowers, trees bobbing
their end of day benediction.

Skaters, cyclers, walkers
busy in their tranquility.
Fullness or emptiness waits
behind closed doors.

Sea lions watching us, watching them
Sea gulls owning the air
show their disdain
by rare baptism upon us.

OREGON

Oregon prizes its outdoor green.
More precious to them than gold.
Their forests indeed are lushly green,
and so, my dear, is their mold.

Sunshine, a rare visitor here.
Constant rain clothes all outdoors.
Nature sings its growing song.
Ferns, trees and fungus spores.

The coastline here only God could make.
It takes your breath away.
Fog rolls in fast, wave pound huge rocks.
Great sunsets end the day.

Their trees do fill your eyes with joy,
with beauty heaven-sent.
No wonder, then each man and child
protects the environment.

Oregonians love their rainy clime!
It doesn't disturb their day.
Best of all, most of all,
it keeps Californians away.

Don't come here they cry with glee.
Stay at your shores, where sunny.
We don't want you moving here.
Just visit, leave your money!

ALASKA

Huge mountains
seeming to push the sky
out of their way.
Clouds resting on mountain brow
sliding down its' side
to rest among trees;
sometimes cloaking mountain top
as if a curtain of privacy
while nature lifts itself
to the heavens in private prayer.
Black, silent mountains
standing quietly
as icy fingers of snow
trace down their crevices.
Here and there a cloud
fell out of the sky and
lays at the foot of a mountain.
Harsh, forbidding climate
ignoring man's intrusion.
Daring you to stay,
challenging you to adjust
for it remains unchanging,
unyielding in its' strength
Summers, a welcome respite.
A time for all to catch their breath
before being buried in snow
once again.
Solitary natures
building cabins hidden in forests.
Needing not wanting not
the fellowship of their brothers.
Cowboy mentality;
bullet holes in all road signs.

Frontiersmen still,
proud of their individuality.
Oilmen, construction workers,
rugged people in a rugged land.
Glaciers, awesome, implacable.
You feel you can't sit
in their presence
out of respect
for these ancient ones.
Frozen crystals of time
daily speaking the unheard
language of the centuries.
Power, pressure encapsulated.
Occasionally breaking forth
with thunderous voice of arrogance,
not caring if it's heard.
An entity unto itself
communing only with
sun, rain, land and sea.
Rivers, lakes, ponds, streams
moving, flowing, dancing
fill the air with
glistening movement of joy
while the rest of nature
stands quietly rooted to the ground.
Waterfalls, the voice of joy
in this land.
Singing Creation's song;
a hymn, to Him.
Sometimes soft,
sometimes loud
as individual arias.
Wildflowers are the laughter of this land.
Brightly, happily
lifting their faces
to the sun, the rain.
The touch-me-not
aura of outdoors
softened with Forget-Me-Nots,

the state flower
Firewood stands
as tiny sentinels
not giving voice
as they watch trespassers.
Noting change, disapprovingly ignoring
guard rails, roads, signs:
Man's "improvements."
Other flowers, names unknown
act as hostesses
waving, greeting, welcoming you
to their world.
The wildlife are
endless treasures here.
Only a land this big
could hold, protect, and hide
the charm, the absolute beauty,
the regal demeanor of bird and beast.
Men trying to wrest a place
for himself here
hasn't caught on
that men should tiptoe upon this land.
For this is a refuge for
some of God's best work
and we are just visitors here.
The mosquito buzzes
it's nervous warning.
Earthquakes, avalanches,
the climate, the vastness
speak louder as nature
tries to tell you
that man will never be in charge here.
For no man can truly own Alaska.

THANKFUL

PRAYER OF THANKSGIVING

Thank you, Lord for my family.
Bless those who have no one to love them.

Thank you, Lord, for my friends.
Bless all those who are lonely.

Thank you, Lord, for my children.
Bless those who have no one to fill their heart,
to make them laugh or drive them crazy.

Thank you, Lord, for my grandchildren.
who fill my heart with joy, laughter and life-affirming emotions..
Bless those who have not had this experience.

Thank you, Lord for my house, my home.
Bless those who have nowhere
to rest their weary head or shelter them

Thank you, Lord, that I have
an abundance of food available to me.
Bless those who go hungry.

Thank you, Lord, for my education.
Bless those who can neither read or write
and are unknowingly starved of the richness of books
or are unaware of the facts and ideas swirling around them.

Thank you, Lord, for my garden.
Bless those who don't have a patch of dirt they can work to bring things alive
and be filled by the beauty of nature.

Thank you, Lord, for You
Bless those who are in poverty of which they are unaware
because they don't know the richness of having You in their lives.

Thank you, Lord, that I am in time, place and space
where I can learn about You and
can grow in that knowledge and love.

THANKFUL?

Yes, thankful that we are in a country where we are able to learn the story and the reality of the Nativity. Thankful we are allowed and are free to learn about God and we can grow in our faith and worship in freedom.

Thankful we have like-minded friends who surround us with love and encourage us to learn. To grow and live life guided by His law, His principles, with morals and values that give our life meaning and purpose.

Thankful that even though we have those decorated trees, Santa Claus, reindeer, Snowmen and "hymns" called Santa Claus Is Coming To Town, Grandma Got Run Over by A Reindeer, etc. we know the real story of the season is a Nativity scene, obedience, miracles, angels and a Saviour. We know where our Saviour really resides: in our hearts, our minds. We know that our body is a temple of the Holy Spirit. We are further told that we are to serve one another, treat each other with love, compassion with wisdom and with humility.

Thankful for our families even though they are a source of some of our greatest joy, sometimes they're the source of some of our greatest distress, for when our kids hurt, we hurt and there's no way around this.

All of this allows us to meditate and ponder Mary's enormous pain watching and knowing what was happening to her beloved Son. How are we to understand? That this was prophesied (and a sword shall pierce her heart) and therefore intentional. If this horrendous suffering happened to her, can we not move towards the truth that we can never really understand our God? And that, somehow, pain has a purpose. Sorrow and joy from life itself. How can we understand and know that everything our God does has a purpose.

Thankful for the gifts of beauty around us; now understanding "Nature was God's first missionary." Who does not wonder at the beauty and color of the world around us. Even the air around us, the clouds, mountains, flowers, trees animals and on and on. Leaving us to finally understand that everything is from Him, of Him, in Him.

That all is Grace.

FORGIVENESS

FORGIVE, ALL YOU HAVE TO LOSE IS YOUR CHAINS.

Always we carry the burden of our scars
from injuries, caused by other that must be forgiven.
We are our scars, our injuries as much as our successes,
as much as the love we receive.
Your heart may always bear the imprint of the chains of unforgiveness.
If you let these feelings go and are able to go forward
without stumbling over the boulders of bitterness, and
the handicap of sorrow you are freeing yourself.
Unforgiveness is so detrimental, yet consuming that letting
go of those negative thoughts and feelings can be a challenge.
You may think it's impossible.
To achieve this is worth all the work, the struggles,
confusion and effort you may have to put forward.
In my own life I didn't want those people
to have that much power in my life.
Be careful.
Unforgiveness can become who you are.
Forget if you can.
Know and believe that the two – forgiving and forgetting
do not have to be inextricably bound together.
Struggle to separate them.
If you are struggling to forgive, go to God and say,
"Father, I want to forgive because this is what you
want me to do. I know that with Your help
I will be able to do this." Then persevere.
Forgiveness is possible.
Forgetting seems to be a song
that comes to mind now and then
and wants to linger.
Choose another song to listen to.

ELUCIDATE AND MEDITATE

Do we really
Think and pay attention to the Lord's prayer
when we ask
"forgive us our trespasses
as we forgive those who
trespass against us."
Do we contemplate and meditate on
how forgiving others will determine
how we will be forgiven?
Do we *really* want to be forgiven
the same way we forgive others?
We've said and read the prayer
so often that we say it by rote
and don't really think about
the words we are saying.

Take time to say it slowly
and meditate on those words.

It will change your life.

DIVINE JUSTICE

Lord, help me
not only to forgive,
but to forgive completely.
No bitterness.
No anger.
Help me to find perspective
and to realize it's in the past.
It's over!
May I grow in
wisdom, empathy, perspective
and compassion for
the hurts and mountains
they've had to climb and overcome.
Grant me understanding
as to WHY they are
what they are.
There will come a time, I truly believe
that divine justice will reach out
and they will literally feel the pain they have caused me.
And, may I remember
that whatever pain I have caused others,
a time will come when I will feel that exact pain myself.
We are wasting our time when we try to "get even"

VENGEANCE IS MINE saith the Lord.

LORD, I AM BROKEN

Lord, help us to forgive those who have broken out hearts.
We lift our children up to you and wonder
if this tragedy in my life has broken their lives too.
I'm in such pain, Lord and I know You understand.
I know You care.
I pray these wounds, these scars bring me closer to You
or what is the purpose of me enduring all this?
Hold onto me.
Your Word tells me that
"all things work to the good for those who love the Lord."
I know this verse and I accept it, Lord, but I am shattered.
I can't make sense of this wounding.
Hold onto me, Lord, I have no strength.
Hold onto me, Lord, just hold me.
Hold me near, just hold me, never let me go.

(Life is not meant to be Endurance contest.)

I'VE BEEN THINKING

WHEN DID YOU KNOW?

Dear Jesus:

When you took that first step,
and left the Father's side,
humbling yourself in total obedience
and became Man,
when did you know who you really were?
When were You really aware
that You were Deity in human form?
When did You know who You really were?
In the womb? Now that's a fascinating thought.
It seems, to me, not as an infant;
Did you go through 'the terrible twos?
Now, ***that*** boggles the mind!
Was it as you reached the age
for being responsible for Your words?
It seems that, when You taught in the Temple,
that You were then aware You were the Son of God.
As Joseph taught You this craft of carpentry
You, who are all-knowing,
who brought all into Creation by Your words,
were You really learning this craft as a child
or presenting a façade
to fit in, to bring forth the Father's intention?

I asked my Spiritual Adviser
and he said "there are multiple schools of thought about this."
It's really fascinating to learn,
to meditate upon, to ponder on the precious years
You spent among us here on earth in bodily form.

As a child, I thought it would be so absolutely wonderful
when we went to Heaven if we could go to a movie theater
and see a film that took 33 years to watch and we could see every
single moment in the life if our Saviour.

ONLY WITH YOU

We are so small in
our Mercy, Compassion and our Love.
How can we understand You?
Lord of ALL,
Lord of the Universe,
how can we begin to understand You
and
fully appreciate You.
O, Prince of Peace
when we quarrel and kill our neighbors
with gossip and criticism
give us understanding that we are
as those who go to war and
bring rebellion, disease and death.
We, who should walk together,
hand in hand toward You.
Always toward You.
To receive Your blessings
and Your peace.
Opening our arms in love
to all our brothers and sisters.
Your beauty,
your beauty we cannot fully see
because we are too small.
Our greatness lies in You,
with You, through You.
Only walking on your path, following You
may we begin to achieve holiness,
to achieve all encompassing love.
Only as we follow you,
can we achieve holiness.

COMING TO UNDERSTAND THE HOLY SPIRIT

How is it, Holy Spirit
that you reside
in all of us.
Do you leave
if you are not heard?
Do you stay
when hearts are not open
to Your whispered,
yet commanding teaching,
Do you stay around us like
say .... a cloak of smoke
waiting for our hearts to open,
to be aware?
You seem to have
no shape, no form.
No physical substance.
Yet you are part of the Trinity,
revealing the great "I Am."
I feel that if,
rather than being able to touch You,
if I was in Your presence, that
instead
You would be in, around
and part of me.
And indeed, our bodies are the temple
of the Holy Spirit.

A GOD SO IN LOVE WITH US

King of Kings
and Lord of Lords,
Creator of all in the Universe
that is seen and unseen by man.
A Holy God
whose holiness and goodness is so immeasurable
that we, your lowly creatures,
cannot look upon your face lest we die.
A being so Holy that our limited hearts and minds
would shrivel and die when faced with
Your Goodness, Your Love
that shines so brightly that, if compared to the Sun,
the Sun would dim in shame.
So you created in us a Soul
where the Holy Spirit dwells
and is there to teach and guide us
if only we accept You and deign to listen.
Our lives, a nano-second long in view of Eternity
where we learn and purify before we stand
before the Throne of Grace.
Here we prepare, though we never become worthy,
to take our place beside the Angels and Saints
to worship and glorify God.
A God so in love with us He wants us with Him in Heaven.
We have proved ourselves so unworthy
that God, the Father, gave His only SON
in a profound and breathtaking way
to be a sacrifice to gain for us
the privilege of living with God forever.

John 3:16
For God so loved the world
He gave his only begotten Son,
so that we would never die.

SILENCE

Silence is not always
merely the absence of sound.
Sometimes it is the sound of Grief
being wrapped in thick layers
as your Soul seems to be smothered
by Despair.
Silence is not always the absence of sound.
At times it is the awful hush of accepting Death.
Silence is not always the absence of sound.
Sometimes it is being so surrounded
by the love of God, for the love of God
that all else is stayed and that any thought,
that strays from Him is unacceptable.
Sometimes the absence of silence
would be intrusive upon a glorious moment.
Sometimes silence is a withdrawing
as all within flees from reality
that is too painful to deal with.
Sometimes it's despair so deep
that it cannot be heard.
Sometimes it's acknowledgement
of despair that it is so deep
it seems as if the Universe has hushed.
Silence is not always the absence of sound
Sometimes it is being so surrounded
by the love of God, for the Love of God
that all else is stayed; that any thought
any action would be as trespassing
into your deepest being.

LABELING PEOPLE

The image is so painful, Lord.
Crown of Thorns
pressed down into your head
in mockery.
The ugliness of the sheer hatefulness.
The spitting, the slaps, blows.
A bloody flogging
which tore strips of flesh
from your precious body.
This was done to You!
You, who are worthy of all Praise.
The final indignity,
a mocking, sarcastic
sign placed above His head
"KING OF THE JEWS"
Little did they know
He was King of Kings
and
Lord of Lords.
Their Creator, Redeemer.

We think "this is all so awful!"
But, how often do we attach a label on others
metaphorically
placing a sign above their head,
to reduce respect for them.

LIGHT

Jesus is the "Light of the World."
It's a Light we don't always see.
We block this Light and stumble through Darkness.
(How stupid, how pitiful are we?")

A blessing of riches we pass right by.
Looking away from the Light.
We peer into Darkness, cling to the belief.
That's what's wrong can't be made right.

Each one of us makes a difference.
Raise your voice, uplift your thoughts.
We can be **Light,*** we can be **Salt.***
In the morass of sin we need not be caught.

We're not helpless and we matter.
We can and should stand tall.
Do unto others, *not* as they do.
Love is important, Love is all.

MT: 5:13 You are the salt of the earth
MT: 5:14 You are the light of the world

COMMUNING WITH GOD

Our hearts converse when spoken words falter.
How to put into words all You've taught and are teaching me?
I know emotions and/or feelings are not essential to belief.
But, at times, they are the only language we seem to be able to use.
If faith were a train, emotions and feelings would
not be the engine, but the caboose.
Faith seems to travel on Grace, Intellect and Commitment
and understood not so much as by our head but our heart.
It seems to be necessary to be bi-lingual in a manner of speaking:
a head-heart synergy.
This communication with You is by Grace and
acknowledgement of hunger to fill those empty places that are
sometimes unrecognized by the spiritual anorexic.
And it's our Soul not our Body that shrivels and shrinks
and can be lead to Spiritual Death.
The more we understand the deeper we fall in
Love with You.
Ours hearts fill, our hearts yearn for Your return,
though we do understand that You are with us always,*
but we long for You so.
Lessons are laid before us and at times
we need to fight through, to persevere, to be victorious.

Be strong and never give up.
If we seek Him we will find.

Scripture speaks:

MT: 28:20
And surely I will be with you always to the very end of the age.

HOLY IS HIS NAME

It seems as if, in this time, that God's name is used as an expletive, a mere expression, more than it is used in prayer. Using these holy names casually. It's sad and disturbing; it's profane. Have we become so lacking in respect, having no respect for anyone or anything that we can treat our Creator with so little appreciation; that we can use His name with scorn, lacking in simple decency and courtesy? Use His name as profanity? He is our loving God, our Father. Jesus called Him Daddy (Abba), an enduring term, denoting a loving being, but we must not forget He is God, He is our Creator, He is so holy that we cannot even look upon His face lest we die. We must treat Him with utmost reverence, devotion, respect and worship.

His name is so holy, so sacred that it should be held in the deepest respect, the highest regard but we use it so casually. We just toss it off with no understanding that we are speaking of the holiest of holies. It really says, "You are nothing. I think of You as nothing, You are not important to me. I doubt you really exist. You mean so little to me, I use your name as an exclamation. The intent may not be to lessen respect for Him but that is the result. We use His holy name in this manner to our own peril (see Bible verses below.) To use His name in this manner is derogatory, disparaging. We degrade and corrupt His name.

I love that the Jews will not speak His name Yahweh, aloud as it is so sacred.

The Fourth Commandment is: **You shall not misuse the name of the Lord, your God for the Lord will not hold anyone guiltless who misuses His name.**

Following are the Bible verses that speak to what I'm trying to convey:

EX 20:7
You shall not misuse the name of the Lord your God, for the Lord will not hold anyone guiltless who misuses His name.

Page 2 HOLY IS HIS NAME

DEUT 5:11

You shall not misuse the name of the Lord, your God, for the Lord will not hold anyone guiltless who misuses His name.

PS 139:20

They speak of You with evil intent, Your adversaries misuse Your name.

....

Blasphemy-the act of expressing lack of reverence for God
Expletive-profane exclamation
Derogatory-intended to lower the reputation of a person or thing
Debase-to lower in character, quality of value
Disparaging-to lower in rank or reputation
Degrading-to lessen from higher to a lower rank
Holy- worthy of absolute devotion
Misuse-to use incorrectly, abuse, mistreat
Profane-impure, defiled, serving to debase what is holy

All these words serve to disrespect and lessen who He is.

LET'S
TALK

KATHRYN'S KWIPS AND KWOTES

Ignorance doesn't have a color.

Sometimes and somehow
we let "The Sword of the Spirit"
become a butter knife!

I really believe it's one of the wonders of the world
that I can talk,
since I so often have my foot in my mouth.

I think that everyone who is
Pro-Abortion
should have to watch one!

Time is precious
and it's a gift.
Be mindful of your moments.

The Sun sets.
The Son is always shining.

Wisdom always trumps Sorry.

I give you so little.
I give you so little, God.
You have been given me eternity,
a glimpse into infinity.
You bought and paid for me.

We can't take back
the things we've done wrong,
but we can make sure
they don't happen again.

Sometimes we fail to see
that our "mission field"
may be in our own home.

In the war
between Good and Evil
old age does not take us out of the fight.

I have learned that,
before God can use us,
we must be humble.
We must get out of our own way.
Otherwise our focus and time
are only on ourselves.

If you can't get what you want,
want what you get!

Amidst all this confusion,
I choose PEACE!

Growing older is wonderful
Now rather than agonize because
I don't have beautiful legs,
I'm so glad I have two of them
and
they both work!

Take a situation
And
Make it an opportunity.

People who drive
80, 90 mph and over
are no longer
in control of their car.
They're just pointing and hanging on!

Dear God,
It seems You're so far.
As near as a whisper,
yet far as a star.

Bless those ahead of us
for they can show us
we still have farther to go.

Bless those who are behind us
for they can show us
how far we have come
and what God has done for us.

-Philippians 3:17, 4:12-14

....

Hate and Resentment
steal pieces of my heart and soul,
leaving me less of a person
than I was meant to be.

....

O Lord, My God
you reside within
where I've been forgiven
and freed from sin.

....

In marriage (among other situations),
it's sometimes more important to be wise
rather than right.
(and sometimes .... Wisdom says shut up!)

....

With all the pain and losses
we bear in our lifetimes,
before you surrender to despair,
consider Mary,

(and a sword shall pierce her heart)

God is bigger than our mistakes.
He's in the business of Restoration.

When looking for love, you must first as yourself-
AM I LOVEABLE?

Want to try to face and solve your problems alone?
(Good luck!)

Jesus, I 'm available!

Dear Jesus,
whatever I was,
You made me more.
You taught me
there was more to be.

I don't know how to say this.
I wish I could say it "nice".
There's just no way to say it:
Sin carries a brutal price.

GOD'S WATCHING:

So ....
I gave you the tools
I gave you the rules.
Now go see what you can do
And, yes, I'm watching!

Everything we do and say
should proclaim the Glory of God

....

Finite can never understand Infinite
but I would like to be able
to appreciate You more.

....

We have to magnify the Lord
with prayer and praise until we grasp
that He is bigger than our problems.

....

As I grow older and I find that bits and pieces of me
don't work as well as they once did.
I now realize that this body is only a "temporary shelter."

....

I think I've finally figured it out,
Lord.
The only way to thank you
is through OBEDIENCE.

....

O Lord, My God
you reside within
where I've been forgiven
and freed from sin.

The Bible says:
"TRIBULATIONS MAKETH YOU PATIENT"
Haven't there been times
in your life when …
Tribulations just "madeth" you tired?

As we serve and
love our neighbor
we are turning
our lives into prayer..

ENCOURAGE.
Don't condemn.
LOVE.
Don't point a finger and tell others
what they're doing wrong.

Do not let the heart of man
tiptoe away
from the presence of God.

When there is real love, committed love,
sex becomes the highest form of communication
Think what you say without words.

Pray twice
before you
speak once.
Or
Pray twiceth
before thou
speaketh onceth,

(sort of a faux King James version)

In the quiet of my
night and day,
my soul does ponder,
my mind does say:
"What is man that you are mindful of him?")

You have to
CHOOSE to
be Happy.

(and sometimes it's hard work!)

Marriage is like the girl with the curl
in the middle of her forehead.
When it's good
it's very, very good
and
when it's bad
it's HORRID.

My motto when I am in danger of being overwhelmed:
YOU CAN ONLY DO, WHAT YOU CAN DO.
Sounds so simple as to need not be expressed,
but I can't believe how these words have helped others
and calms them down.

ASK!
All anyone can say is No!

Oh yes, we are quite clever.
Thinking we know all that we know.
But, look around you and see what's happening.
You REAP what you SOW.

Watching the news:
You understand that
it's not against the law
to be stupid.

The MARTHA COMPLEX:
I can get so busy
DOING
that I don't have time for
BECOMING

As we do, we become.
Do God's will
and
He'll take care of the rest.
Philippians 4:9

I once had a friend who wouldn't go to church
because of all the sinners she saw sitting there on Sundays.
She said they all were a bunch of hypocrites.
I told her that that's exactly where Sinners should be.

(Neither one of us was convinced by the other.)

Remember,
the sun and the SON
are always there
to bring light
into the darkness.

Oh dear, I've had it confirmed
that we are not so wise.
We say, "Jesus, rule over our problems,
but not over our lives!"

As you act,
so you shall become

Come grow old with me,
stanza of the old, love poem:
the best is yet to be."
(Where are we going next, Lord?)

....

Life is not meant
to be
an endurance contest.

....

The Love of my Life
is gone
and the world is less of a place to be.

....

I Think it's just WONDERFUL
that some people have their lives so in order
that they can tell you how to run your life!
It's just *WONDERFUL!!*

(Sarcasm can be SO satisfying)

....

You reach down and lift us up.
You come to us
through "bread and cup."
We come to you
through prayer and thought,
You give us all;
all that we've sought.

....

May I die in good health.

(Think about it-in a few minutes it will begin
to make good sense.) ....

....

I'm Wondering ...
When you get to Heaven, do you get to know
where all those socks are that
the dryer ate? .... .Just wondering.

....

Being single:
There's nobody to bother you.
There's no buddy either.

....

What a surprising revelation
when came the realization
that some people never grow up
.... they just grow old.

....

I'm gonna take my fears
and Me and my Fears
are gonna do it!

....

There are circumstances
over which I have no control.
I CAN choose how I feel about the situation.

....

In my 40's
I loved children
but NOT in my house.

Then, in my 50's
I felt that God's idea of dessert
is grandchildren.

Out in this busy, noisy world
we must find Quiet Time.
Time to think and let our thoughts meander.
To look at who we are what we are
and
who and what we are becoming.
Quiet is the life blood of
Growing, Maturing and Excellence.

I began to wonder if anyone used the word
"INTEGRITY"
anymore or even if the word is understood!
(I even checked my dictionary to make sure it's still in there!)

Guard your thoughts.
They are important.
Even your thoughts can imprint on your Soul.
Be mindful.

A kind word is never lost.
It's under the headings of:
Encouragement,
Loving your neighbor.
Loving Kindness.
You create your own space around you
by an optimistic outlook
and taking the fleeting moments
to see the goodness in people.

Being a Grandmother,
I realize that my
biggest blessings
are "little ones!"

We do not have a promise that tomorrow will come.
Or even that we will have the rest of today.
So be careful and use the next minutes, hours, days
in a positive and loving way.

We've all got something in our past, our lives
that we wouldn't want seen on that big T.V. Screen "up there!"

As I grow older, Lord,
keep my heart tender
lest with the passing years
it grows brittle and breaks and crumbles away.

Lord,
help all those who think
the world revolves around *them*,
rather than the Sun.

Take a situation
and make it an opportunity.

Dear Jesus
Whatever I was,
You made me more.
You taught me
there was more to be

When the Bible is held up for all to see
before the Gospel message
I feel that even tho' I have a Bible at home
I can't seem to take my eyes off His Word
when I am in His House.
I think it's a reminder
to never take my eyes off Him.
Such a lovely reminder.

I love, love, love Thomas Edison's last words:
"It's very beautiful over there!"

Words of wisdom for our weary world
and especially the Middle East:
Mohatmas Ghandi said:
Why would I kill a man
when I only want to change his mind?

....

I think that if we feel that we've got GOD
all figured out and that we understand,
then we need to be very worried.

....

A friend, who has been going through a litany of difficulties,
said to me:
What is God trying to tell me?
I answered:
He's saying "What will it take to get your attention?"

....

I really don't want to carry around
unforgiveness, anger, hurt.
I call it emotional garbage
and
you know what happens to garbage
if you keep carrying it around!

....

Is the rose important because of its beauty, its fragrance?
Or just because it is the work of His hands?

....

We're always learning something new.
What's exciting most of all:
When we think we understand God,
we always make Him too small!

....

These are some days, Lord that I feel
the only goodness in me … is You!

....

Isn't it heartbreaking to realize
that for some of us
our lives are often filled with:
"shoulda, coulda, woulda?"

....

The Bible is the only "How To" Book
that doesn't have a self-help section.

....

Watching the news ....
It seems as if the shortest distance between two points
is that between an index finger and a trigger.

....

There have been spiritually beautiful moments in my life
when I've felt as if I was unmistakably walking in
"Son-shine"..

....

If, in your Life,
you can positively touch one other Life, or many lives,
then your Life will have been worthwhile.
How can you ask for more?

....

Aren't there days,
and even hours
when you think, you feel
that God didn't get "the Memo?"

But remember, He promised
"I will be with you always."
Sometimes His plans
are not what we think we want.

....

I know enough
to know
that I don't know enough.

....

You are the Creator of the Universe,
of man in all his complexities.
As you teach me, I struggle for understanding.
Achieving tiny steps forward
as my journey, so profound continues.
Exciting is my journey.

....

Medea was a mythological figure
who killed her own children.
Sound familiar?
It seems as if personal responsibility
has always been a problem.

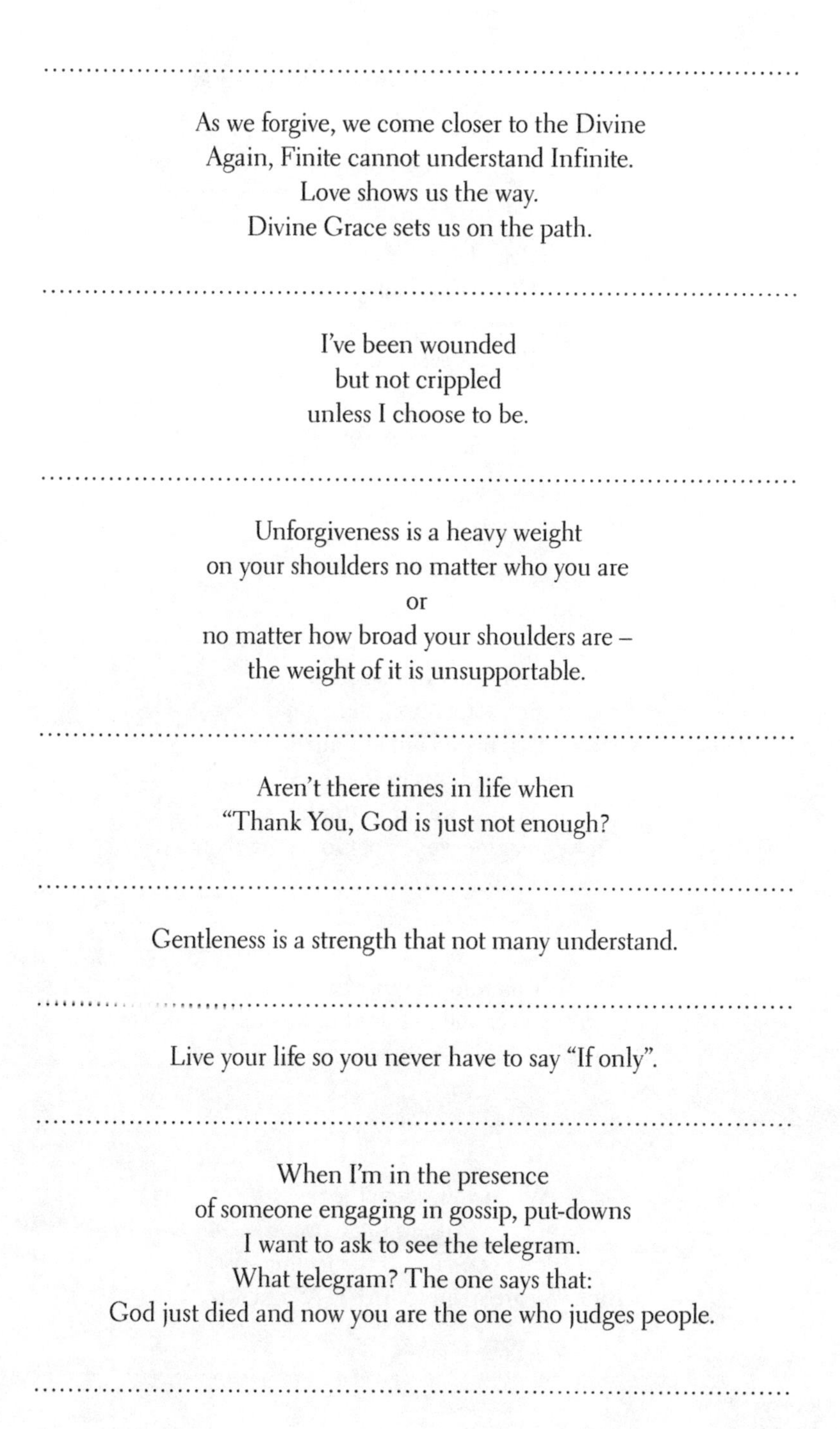

As we forgive, we come closer to the Divine
Again, Finite cannot understand Infinite.
Love shows us the way.
Divine Grace sets us on the path.

I've been wounded
but not crippled
unless I choose to be.

Unforgiveness is a heavy weight
on your shoulders no matter who you are
or
no matter how broad your shoulders are –
the weight of it is unsupportable.

Aren't there times in life when
"Thank You, God is just not enough?

Gentleness is a strength that not many understand.

Live your life so you never have to say "If only".

When I'm in the presence
of someone engaging in gossip, put-downs
I want to ask to see the telegram.
What telegram? The one says that:
God just died and now you are the one who judges people.

Oh, my Lord, my God – who or what would
fill the holes in me if you weren't in my life?

Oh dear, I've had it confirmed
That we are not so wise.
We say, "Jesus, rule over our problems,
But not over our lives!"

As you act,
so shall you become.

When I think I understand God
something, somehow makes me realize
I've made Him too small.
5 years later, I read this in my church bulletin:
It's for the best we err in thinking most
when we imagine we've got God figured out.

We have to magnify the Lord
with prayer and praise until we grasp
that He is bigger than our problems.

When you watch the news
(or even drive to LAX airport)
don't you just get the feeling
that you are in an INSANE ASYLUM?

Instead of telling God what we want,
try asking God what He wants.
(Then stand back)

....

I was looking at my Bible
And began to wonder,
Is your Life bound by Gilt or Guilt?

....

Suffering seems to teach us Humility.
(or we whine and complain and
no one can stand to be with us)

....

Faith is a journey.
Life is a journey.
Pack your baggage carefully.

....

MONEY and SEX are alike.
They're only important
when you haven't got them!
(Some rascal suggested that I add toilet paper to the list!)

....

If nature could speak
MUSIC
would be its' voice.

....

When your hands
are clasped in prayer,
they are halfway
to lifting up to heaven.
They are halfway there
to opening your arms to others.

WALK IN LOVE

Why aren't we just honest
and pray for longer arms
to pat ourselves on the back
When we do
something wunnnnderful?

I AM
Is the reason
I am.

We don't need to be
PERFECT
for God to use us.
We only have to be
WILLING.

I just know that someday
they are going to scientifically prove that:
LONELINESS CAUSES BRAIN DAMAGE.
(Especially when I think of some of the dates I went on.)

Once you totally understand
that God, as Creator,
is the source of all things –
it's so easy to thank Him for *Everything*!

....

There are worse things than being single
and
some of them are married to my best friends.

....

It's amazing how many pot-bellied
little boys are "out there."

....

Puzzling about existence
the answer some choose
is that we came from
Primordial Ooze!

(can you *buh-leeve* that?)

....

We carry a child
under our heart
before it is born.
Then we carry
our child
in our heart
All the rest of our lives.

....

Motherhood
begins in labor
and
is hard work from then on!

....

Most of my single girlfriends
have been single for so long
that they no longer refer to "him"
as "Mister Right."
Now they say – "Mr. Good Enough"
or
"Mr. Not So Bad"

....

Time will always move on
presenting its' own challenges
we must cope with and conquer.

Waste not one moment
for you will never have
that particular time again.

....

Take a situation
and
make it an opportunity

....

Was there a reason
they were called Beatitudes
and not
Do-Attitudes?

....

What you don't deal with,
will deal with you.

Here's what I believe
You have to be humble for God to use you.
We are here to learn lessons.
The Hardest lessons teach us the most
And
Ice cream always makes you feel better.

Nature was God's first missionary.

(This is not original to me but I love it.)

I checked my birth certificate
and there are no guarantees
that Life was going to be Easy.
(Or even fair!)

I was just told that babies, from conception,
have their own DNA
So .... it's a separate body!!!!
Hmmmm, that brings up a whole range
of new arguments.

CPSIA information can be obtained
at www.ICGtesting.com
Printed in the USA
BVHW030839100420
577303BV00001B/53